I0125456

The Problem of Order in Changing Societies

The Problem of Order in Changing Societies

Essays on Crime and Policing in
Argentina and Uruguay

Edited by
Lyman L. Johnson

University of New Mexico Press
Albuquerque

Library of Congress Cataloging-in-Publication Data

The problem of order in changing societies : essay on crime and
policing in Argentina and Uruguay / edited by Lyman L. Johnson. —
1st ed.
p.   cm.
Includes bibliographical references.
ISBN 0-8263-1181-4
1. Crimes—Argentina—Buenos Aires—History. 2. Crime—Uruguay-
-History. 3. Police—Argentina—Buenos Aires—History. 4. Police—
Uruguay—History. I. Johnson, Lyman L.
HV6885.B8P76 1990
364.982'11—dc20
89-36709
CIP

© 1990 by the University of New Mexico Press.
All rights reserved.
First edition

ISBN-13: 978-0-8263-1181-8

For Sue

Contents

Preface

Lyman L. Johnson

For Latin America, the historical study of crime and policing exists today as a minor subfield of social history. There was little systematic study of crime and public order in Latin America before historians of Europe and the United States demonstrated clearly the potential of this field. Because Latin Americanists have tended to follow routes marked out by scholars studying other regions, many of the issues and methods currently found in this field are derivative. There are some signs that this is changing as historians have begun to apply Marxist and dependency analyses to this field.[1] At present, however, this revisionist process has produced only limited results. Among the small number of scholarly monographs and a somewhat larger body of journal articles on crime and public order in Latin America, there are a number of excellent studies that illuminate the region's social and economic history in new ways.[2] In a number of cases, studies of historical criminology or the police have won a broader readership by illuminating larger issues of social and economic change. The essays collected in this volume are contributions to this effort.

Despite these achievements, the promise of historical criminology remains largely unfulfilled for Latin America. This is, in large part, the natural result of the thinness of the current literature. In addition, the failure of scholars to link research in ways that would allow the examination of crime and policing over significant time periods or across large geographic areas has tended to limit our ability to make generalizations and develop theory. Two periods clearly lend themselves to this more ambitious research agenda. The bureaucratic and judicial structures of the Spanish colonial order imposed a rough uniformity in statute, enforcement, and record keeping. Colonial historians, therefore, should be able to examine questions of crime and punishment comparatively across a vast area of space and time. Similar opportunities exist for late nineteenth- and twentieth-century research. After 1880, many Latin American governments began to collect and report uniform criminal statistics. Although statutes and enforcement priorities differed from nation to nation, some categories of crime found in these records, homicide and some property crimes for example, can be studied in a comparative fashion. Such studies would help illuminate the social consequences of urbanization, economic development, and internal and international migration.

Visible both in the formulation and enforcement of legal codes are a society's assumptions about racial, ethnic, and gender relations; family and household organization; child-rearing practices; and class structure. In statutes we find the idealized values of a society. In the actions of police and courts we find vernacular custom. Common crimes such as drunkenness, disorderly conduct, and, in our time, marijuana use are defined more by police practice than by statute. When confronted by dramatic changes in arrest rates for these misdemeanors, then, we need to identify both the circumstances that led to altered enforcement priorities and changes in the social context. There is even a subjective dimension to the enforcement of some felony statutes, despite the costly and time-consuming judicial scrutiny of police action in these cases. In order to explain changes in crime rates or arrest rates over time, an effort must be made to specify contemporary changes both in the behavior of police and courts and in social norms. Historical criminology requires the careful elaboration of the political and social context.

There is widespread belief that changes in economic structure or in class relations lead to changes in crime levels. The evidence, however, is somewhat ambiguous. Increased crime rates, especially rates of property crime, are commonly associated in the literature with urbanization. Changes in the age distribution of the population are also tied to the crime rate. Younger, more masculine populations generally produce higher rates. More developed industrialized nations have relatively higher property crime rates and lower personal crime rates than lesser-developed nations. The business cycle, however, does not appear to be a good predictor of crime rates, or more accurately, the connections are not what researchers at first assumed. In the U.S., for example, rates fell in the depressed 1930s and rose in the expansive 1960s.[3] Economic variables seem to gain explanatory power only when researchers closely control for age, gender, and other characteristics of the population. In this area, Latin Americanists are disadvantaged by limitations in available economic and demographic research.

This book offers six essays on crime and public order in the Río de la Plata region. Five of the essays examine various criminological issues in the history of Argentina and one is devoted to Uruguay. As is common in other areas of the region's historiography, the city of Buenos Aires and its immediate hinterland dominate this book and, more generally, the field of historical criminology. Given the demographic, economic, and political weight of Buenos Aires, this emphasis is predictable, even necessary. An evaluation of how the region's social and economic diversity affected the definition and enforcement of acceptable behavior is further provided by John Chasteen's study of rural violence in Uruguay and by Karla Robinson and Richard Slatta's examination of the Buenos Aires countryside during the early nineteenth century. My comparative study of arrest rates for Buenos Aires, Santa Fe, and Tucumán during the period from 1900 to 1930 also explores how differences in population size, ethnic origins, and levels of economic development affected crime rates.

It is not mere coincidence that both the scientific study of crime and the creation of new institutions for the apprehension and punishment of criminals appeared first in the most dynamic commercial and industrial nations. The development of modern police departments in Europe and North America occurred only after the appearance of new, politically assertive, propertied classes that demanded increased protection and a more orderly society.[4] The evidence seems to suggest that crime rates, particularly rates for violent crime, fell throughout Europe and North America from the late nineteenth century to the post-World War II period.[5] There is disagreement among scholars about the origins of these changed levels of crime, but most are willing to grant increased law-enforcement efforts some of the credit.

Rates of banditry and other forms of crime and disorderliness seem to have risen throughout Latin America during the tumultuous decades after independence, when they were seen nearly everywhere as an obstacle to commerce and investment. As a result, public order became one of the key objectives for the more vigorous and resolute central governments that were in place nearly everywhere by the 1890s. Those nations that proved most successful in pursuing export-led development moved quickly to imitate the institutions and practices found in London, Paris, and New York. Police training, criminal statistics, prison architecture, and even juvenile statutes were brought into agreement with established practice in industrial nations. The new social science of criminology also found a small but enthusiastic audience in Latin America.

In the Río de la Plata region, the ambitions of those charged with the maintenance of public order grew with available resources. As the agricultural economy expanded in the decades leading up to World War I, Buenos Aires, Montevideo, and many provincial capitals in the region added police manpower, improved police training, introduced new crime detection methods, and sought new technologies—such as fingerprinting, motorcycles, and automobiles—that would improve criminal apprehension rates and shorten police reaction time. This was a costly business, but wide support existed across much of the political landscape. Only among syndicalists and anarchists was this enthusiasm for order seen as oppressive and inherently antidemocratic. Although the modernization of law enforcement progressed rapidly after WWI, even in the countryside, we can locate the antecedents of this process as early as the late colonial period, when efforts were made to expand rural constabularies and urban night patrols.

The Río de la Plata region experienced a revolution in economic organization and social structure during the period covered by these essays. Beginning in the late colonial period, the region's agricultural and grazing sectors were increasingly tied to markets in Europe, Brazil, and Cuba, although the full potential of this expansion was not realized until the last decades of the nineteenth century. Then, improvements in transportation, the introduction of refrigeration, and a massive wave of European immigration combined to allow the region's meat and grain producers to compete successfully with North American exporters for the European market. When examined in terms of aggregate economic statistics, the results were impressive. Both Argentina and Uruguay pulled ahead of most other Latin American nations in per capita gross domestic product as well as in other standard measures of economic progress. Wages in both countries, in fact, reached European levels. The fruits of this expansion were experienced unevenly across the class structure and from region to region, however. The largest urban centers benefited more than did small towns and the countryside. The littoral grew rich while the interior lagged behind. In class terms, the landowning elite and urban middle class were the major beneficiaries of new prosperity, while the urban and rural working classes received a declining share of the wealth.

The maturation of the export economy coincided with political consolidation in both Argentina and Uruguay. Improvements in transportation and enhanced fiscal resources provided the means finally to overcome residual opposition to strong central government in the provinces. National political integration, though, was accomplished with great difficulty, and the period from 1890 to World War I witnessed numerous political risings and rebellions. Despite resistence, however, central authority expanded inexorably. Bureaucracy subsumed traditional mechanisms of patronage and clientelism, thus tying local authorities more directly to national governments.

Relative political stability and expanding economies in turn induced accelerated levels of foreign investment and immigration. By the eve of World War I, there were few visible survivals of the colonial past. Perhaps the best single measure of the scale of this transformation is provided by the growth of the regional metropolis, Buenos Aires. From a city of approximately 50,000 in 1810, the capital celebrated the centennial of independence in 1910 with 1.5 million inhabitants.

These profound changes in economic and political organization had important social consequences for the region. Beginning with the rationalization of the grazing industry in the early national period, conflicts occurred between the region's landowning class and the rural masses. Enhanced export opportunities highlighted the chronic problem of inadequate labor supply. Landowners reacted by creating severe vagrancy laws and expanding rural police resources to help provide a more disciplined and reliable work force. The punitive nature of these policies contributed to high levels of rural violence.

New technologies that permitted the profitable export of chilled and frozen meat further altered social structure. Employers promoted immigration to overcome labor shortages, arguing that immigrant workers were also more productive and better disciplined than the native-born. These new export products also called into being a more diversified occupational structure that included greater levels of specialization and a more highly stratified distribution of income.

At each stage of this transformation, the coercive powers of the police and the courts were used to protect property, maintain public order, and provide a disciplined work force. Both statute and judicial practice were employed to affirm the authority of parents over children, husbands over wives, and employers over workers. In addition, the police and courts commonly worked to maintain the existing conventions of the social hierarchy. Wealthy men and women demanded that the police and courts protect them from the verbal or physical assaults of their social inferiors. Deference, as well as labor discipline, was enforced by police power.

The increasingly self-confident elites of the region's cities sought to sanitize society by attacking traditionally tolerated evils such as prostitution and begging. The concept of progress, commonly defined in the terms of European societies, often proved a useful tool for limiting the freedom and independence of the working masses. As the efficiency and resources of government grew, foot patrols, improved training practices, crime labs, and other crime-fighting tools were created as quickly as budgets permitted. The crowded housing precincts of the working class were targeted for an increased police presence. New, nontraditional, responsibilities were also given to the police and the courts. By 1914, the concern for order led to an expansion of police and judicial authority to include the inspection of housing, the enforcement of public hygiene, and the care of lost children.

Each of the contributors to this volume has placed the discussion of crime and public order within the larger context of changing social and economic structures. They have not made a systematic effort to explore the individual origins of criminal and other anti-social behaviors. Instead, the primary concern has been an examination of the social order and cultural value system within which criminality was defined and punished. Where possible an effort was made to periodize changes in the incidence of criminal behavior as measured by arrests or convictions. Given the limitations in the historical record, however, conclusions about actual levels of criminality and orderliness are necessarily tentative.

Susan Socolow examined all surviving decisions by colonial courts of the first instance for criminal cases where women were either victims or perpetrators. The forty-year period covered by her study witnessed Buenos Aires's emergence as the major regional entrepôt and political center. This was also a period of remarkable demographic growth during which the city's population increased by a factor of three. As the city's population grew, crimes involving women increased as well, with the greatest increase visible after 1777.

Socolow carefully discriminates among social and racial groups in her analysis and finds poor women in general more vulnerable. Nearly all the crimes involving women of the urban working class were of a sexual nature. The most common were wife-beating, rape, kidnapping, and assault. In many cases, women in the colonial city were victims of assaults and sexual attacks intended to humiliate their fathers or husbands. As is still common today, the perpetrators were generally known to their victims. They were husbands, family members, and neighbors. Home was one of the most dangerous places for women in colonial Buenos Aires.

Acts of violence were commonly precipitated when males believed that a woman had somehow overstepped customary norms by word or deed. Direct challenges to male authority, especially the authority of a husband or father, could provoke violence. As a result, judges scrutinized the behavior of the victim with great care. If the woman's behavior was seen as provocative or scandalous, the perpetrator was seldom punished, even when injury occurred.

Perhaps the most startling discovery Socolow presents is the relatively mild punishments the courts gave to perpetrators. Although statute law, religious teachings, and literary commentary from this society suggest that the protection of female honor was a central concern, this analysis informs us that there was a clear class dimension to its implementation. Only women of the propertied classes could depend on the legal system to protect them from violence and insults.

Richard Slatta and Karla Robinson explore the criminal justice system of the Province of Buenos Aires during 1820–50, a period of great political violence and instability. This was also a time of economic expansion, as pampean livestock producers found new and vigorous markets for exports of hides, salted meat, and other animal products. Traditionally historians have viewed the dictatorship of Juan Manuel de Rosas, which lasted from 1829 to 1852, as a social and economic watershed. The triumph of Rosas is commonly used to mark the final eclipse of the commercial and bureaucratic classes that had dominated the city of Buenos Aires and much of the viceroyalty in the late colonial era. In the place of the old elite there appeared an ascendant class of rural landowners. Whether Rosas is portrayed as a nationalist hero or dictatorial villain, his regime is generally viewed as dissimilar in both class basis and social policy from those of his Unitarian predecessors.

Robinson and Slatta find, in contrast to this view, fundamental continuity both in the definition and punishment of crime. Throughout the period 1820–50, the courts and police were used to protect and promote the interests of the propertied classes. Well before Rosas's rise to power, the statutes and judicial practices of the Unitarian period had already circumscribed the liberty of the rural working class, setting the stage for a more complete repression under Rosas. Internal passports and antivagrancy laws limited freedom of movement and required employment. Those who attempted to evade these laws were forced into the army or were jailed.

The data from early nineteenth-century Argentina is in general agreement with what is known about other preindustrial nations. There was a generally high level of crime, and violent crimes were more common than property crimes. Those arrested by the police, both in the city and in the countryside, were usually young males from the working class. As Socolow found for the colonial city, punishment was generally lenient, although some brutal sentences were also imposed.

Rural violence is also the theme of John Chasteen's essay. Using a more anthropological approach, he examines the social and economic context for masculine violence in nineteenth-century Uruguay. Why did these men fight? What provoked these often-deadly contests that were so typical of this society? Chasteen is able to provide convincing answers to these and other questions by examining closely a number of duels. Court records provide a richly detailed summary of these terrible events. The physical and verbal provocations often had a highly ritualized character. Fighting was an important part of masculine culture. Among men with little wealth, personal honor was tenaciously guarded. No man could receive an insult without devaluing his name and losing the respect of his neighbors and workmates. Although some men from the propertied classes participated in these violent contests, knife duels were primarily a means whereby the gauchos established their own social hierarchy.

Donna Guy's study of prostitution and female criminality is a major contribution to twentieth-century Argentine social history as well as an original contribution to historical criminology. Her study of changing public policy toward prostitution in Buenos Aires also sheds important new light on the politics of this crucial period. Urban authorities altered their policies toward prostitution in response to changes in the level and character of immigration, to changes in the city's housing stock, and to changes in female work force participation. They also responded to the pressures of local political and economic interest groups.

In addition, the campaign against prostitution provided a convenient venue for ideological debate. At root, however, the framing and enforcement of prostitution statutes were tied to the question of women's rights. Although campaigns against prostitution commonly proclaimed a desire to protect women and sustain the family, they were in practice justifications to harass and humiliate women while protecting male clients and pimps. Professor Guy's explanation of the economic context of this illegal commerce is particularly helpful in understanding the shifting context of law and enforcement. Limited economic opportunities and salary discrimination played a significant role in the recruitment of prostitutes. It was the failure of reformers adequately to address this motivation that doomed their efforts.

Julia Blackwelder provides an analysis of arrest rates for the city of Buenos Aires in the period from 1880 to 1914. She places the city's experience in a comparative context by using data drawn from studies of cities in the United States. She argues that this comparison is justified by similarities in size, educational levels, immigration patterns, and occupational mix. She finds that Buenos Aires diverged significantly from the North American model.

The large cities of the United States experienced a decline in the incidence of both property crime and violent crime from the middle of the nineteenth century to the 1950s. In Buenos Aires, both forms of felony crime remained high. She finds the possible explanation for this difference in the absence of "a fully developed industrial economy that supported the upward mobility and increasingly stable employment of the urban working classes in the United States." Blackwelder also suggests that the tardy development of other urban centers in Argentina reduced employment opportunities and exacerbated the effects of cyclical contractions in the economy of Buenos Aires. Unlike felony arrests, misdemeanor arrests fell throughout this period as they did in the United States. The author suggests that this resulted largely from changes in police priorities and in altered housing patterns.

My comparative analysis of three Argentine cities extends Blackwelder's investigation of Buenos Aires to 1930 and includes two interior cities never before examined systematically, Santa Fe and Tucumán. I explore the possible connections between crime and levels of economic development as manifested in occupational mix, literacy levels, and ethnic origins. Both misdemeanor and felony arrest rates were calculated and compared for the three cities. Data on homicide and suicide for Buenos Aires and Tucumán are also presented. The experiences of these three Argentine cities are compared with selected European and North American cities.

As was true in Blackwelder's study of Buenos Aires in an earlier period, arrest patterns in all three cities diverge from the pattern established in studies of cities in more industrialized societies. As a result, standard criminological theory does not adequately explain the Argentine case. The tendencies predicted by theory failed to appear. Violent crime rates did not decline after 1900 and property crime rates did not trend upward. Although the origin of the Argentine pattern cannot be asserted with complete confidence, I suggest that the occupational structure of this agricultural exporting economy, in particular the necessary fluidity of the work force, played a determining role in sustaining both high levels of violent crime and high suicide levels. Despite Argentina's relative prosperity in the period before the Great Depression, its high wage levels, and high incidence of literacy, the nation retained in fundamental ways the social characteristics of its less developed past.

These essays represent a modest contribution to the study of crime and public order. There is much work to be done. The authors suggest some likely directions for future research and identify a broad range of new sources that have been little used before. The uniform statistical reports published by municipal authorities, in particular, appear to hold significant promise for future research. If we hope to learn more about the process of social change in Latin America by examining crime and deviance, then we are obligated to trace these issues over lengthy periods. Some of the benefits of this longer perspective are observable here, particularly in fixing the relationship between changing levels of personal and property crime and alterations in social and economic organization; Problems, however, abound. Changes in political and bureaucratic organization as well as changes in statute make the estimation of long-term trends difficult. Despite these difficulties and challenges, the authors hope that these essays will attract new scholars to this field. We look forward to the discussions and debates that will follow.

Notes

1. One recent example of this revisionist tendency is Martha Knisely Huggins, *From Slavery to Vagrancy in Brazil* (New Brunswick, N.J., 1984). A good first introduction to this point of view is found in William J. Chambliss and Milton Mankoff, *Whose Law? Whose Order? A Conflict Approach to Criminology* (New York, 1976).

2. A general survey is not appropriate here. I believe William B. Taylor's *Drinking, Homicide and Rebellion in Colonial Mexican Villages* (Stanford, 1979) to be among the most successful historical treatments of crime and disorder in Latin America. Paul J. Vanderwood's *Disorder and Progress: Bandits, Police, and Mexican Development* (Lincoln, 1981) is clearly among the most useful of the studies of the postindependence period.

3. P. J. Cook and G. A. Zarkin, "Crime and the Business Cycle," *Journal of Legal Studies* 14:1 (Jan. 1985): 115–28. For a similar analysis of the British experience, see K. I. Wolpin, "An Economic Analysis of Crime and Punishment in England and Wales, 1894–1967," *Journal of Political Economy* (Oct. 1978): 815–40.

4. This process is well summarized for the United States in Erick H. Monkkonen, *Police in Urban America, 1860–1920* (Cambridge, 1981). Ted Robert Gurr, "Crime Trends in Modern Democracies since 1945," *Inter-*

national Annals of Criminology, 16: 2 (1977): 41–86. See also James Q. Wilson and Richard J. Herrnstein, *Crime and Human Nature* (New York, 1985), especially chapter 16, "Historical Trends in Crime," pp. 407–438.

5. M. J. Hindelang, M. R. Gottfredson, and T. J. Flanagan, *Sourcebook of Criminal Justice Statistics* (Washington, D.C., 1981). For evidence of a similar periodization in Great Britain, consult F. H. McClintock and N. H. Avison, *Crime in England and Wales* (London, 1968).

1

Women and Crime

Buenos Aires, 1757–97

Susan Migden Socolow

Crime reflects social values, for it indicates what is viewed as abnormal or deviant behavior (and conversely what is acceptable behavior) and the degree to which that behavior is abhorrent to society in general. In addition to reflecting general values, crime, insofar as it involves one racial, sexual, or social group, can shed light on the attitude of the ruling elite toward a specific group and the social position of that group within a larger context. Last, crime reflects class and power relations by allowing us to study the relationship of the criminal to the victim and their relationship to the legal mechanism. The study of crime as a valid field for historical research has been well explored by European historians, but within the field of Latin American history it is relatively new.[1] It is, nevertheless, an area deserving of study in our attempt to understand more fully colonial Spanish society.

The few studies in Latin American history that have to date touched on the problem of crime and punishment have generally looked at illegal behavior as it affected non-Spanish groups.[2] This study is concerned with criminal behavior and crime as it affected women, both Spanish and non-Spanish, in late eighteenth-century Buenos Aires. A study of women and crime allows us to view the role of women in colonial society, as well as to test colonial society's preceptions of sex roles and the way men and women actually behaved.[3] Moreover, cases concerning criminal law demonstrate how markedly practices could differ from written statutes, and how class, sex, and race served to modify the law as it applied to different individuals.[4]

To study the pattern of crimes in which women were either victims or perpetrators, criminal cases brought before courts of the first instance for the area under the jurisdiction of the city of Buenos Aires were reviewed.[5] The cases under study cover a forty-year period in colonial Argentine history, a period in which Buenos Aires and the surrounding countryside underwent dynamic economic and population growth as the city became a center of commercial and administrative activity. This study purposely stops short of the years of the English invasions, when political chaos and military conditions created a somewhat abnormal social environment. It should be pointed out that the civil and criminal jurisdiction of the city of Buenos Aires covered large rural areas and that many of the crimes reviewed occurred in a rural or semirural setting.

For the lower classes, colonial Buenos Aires was a violent society based on hierarchy and full of conflict situations. The subordination of women was a given of the social order, but there was also subordination of the lower classes and the poor. Although justice was available to all in theory, the records show that, especially in the rural outskirts of the city, justice was often inaccessible and much crime did not come to the attention of the authorities.

Feminine behavior differed greatly from one social group to another and from one racial group to another. The ideal was no doubt that of the Spanish (or white) upper-class female, who led a gracious, albeit sheltered life. Life for these women was often a choice between marriage partners, one mortal, the other divine, although a few upper- and middle-class women remained single. Early marriage was followed by strict rules of decorum and, for those who had chosen an earthly partner, by a rapid succession of offspring. Well-bred women were kept in a state of semi-isolation; their major diversion consisted of churchgoing.

In theory, women of the better classes did not work, but Spanish single women and widows were often forced into some type of economic activity to maintain themselves. The preferred means of earning a livelihood was twofold: renting rooms in one's house while sending out some of one's slaves to work for day wages. Both of these economic activities avoided direct entry into the larger masculine world and were therefore acceptable for the finer class of women. Less passive female economic activity did exist, however, and became more frequent as one went down the social scale. In the urban areas, middle- and lower-class women were found working as teachers, midwives, launderesses, and ironing women. Rural women shared with men the chores of farms and ranches.[6]

At the bottom of the social scale were the female black slaves, who were as active as their male counterparts in the labor market, although they tended to be employed inside the house.

For this study, information was gathered from a total of seventy criminal cases prosecuted in one of the two municipal courts of the city, the *juzgado del alcalde de primer voto* and the *juzgado del alcalde de segundo voto*. All cases involving women, approximately 20 percent of the total 355 cases brought before these judges, were included in the group. This relatively low percentage tends to reinforce the view of colonial women as sheltered individuals who passed their lives outside the public domain. This group of cases does not, unfortunately, contain records from the ecclesiastical courts or the Inquisition, where a large number of cases involving women as plaintiffs or defendants were probably presented.[7] In the case of Buenos Aires, none of these records has survived.

Those records that did survive reflect a growing participation of women in crime, either as plaintiff or defendant, after the founding of the viceroyalty in 1777. The total number of cases involving women found for the twenty-year period before 1777 was sixteen; by contrast, fifty-four cases were found for the twenty-year period after that date. This reflects both an increase in the population of the area and the tightening up of legal practices and institutions after the founding of the viceroyalty. Approximately half the cases studied occurred within the city of Buenos Aires; the other half were crimes committed in an area extending 145 miles from the city and included in the city's legal jurisdiction.

Because of suspected underreporting of crimes involving women, known omissions in the case material reviewed, and haphazard records, this study does not attempt to specify absolute rates or numbers of certain crimes. It is impossible to know how many crimes involving women never came to public attention. Nevertheless, existing criminal records provide a picture of the variety of crime and allow the historian to examine realities and underlying social ideals.

Crime is often divided into three general categories: economic crimes, or those against property, such as robbery, larceny, and theft; interpersonal crimes, or crimes resulting from conflicts between individuals, including homicide, rape, slander, stabbing, and bigamy; and political crimes, or conflicts between individuals and the state, such as treason and lese majesty.[8] Although the records of the city-magistrate courts include multiple examples of so-called economic crimes, almost all crimes involving women fall into the second category, interpersonal crimes. In addition, almost all the crimes that involved women were of a sexual nature.

This lack of female involvement in cases of economic crimes does not prove that colonial *porteña* women never stole or committed larceny. In any society employing a large number of household servants, some petty thievery, for example, will always occur. What is obvious is that if these crimes were committed by or against women, they were never reported, indicating that they were either not considered serious enough to appeal to royal justice for legal redress or that the thief was punished privately. In addition, the lack of female involvement in economic crimes suggests that women were not forced to be economically independent to the same degree as men. Women who found themselves in need of economic support could enter into illicit sexual relationships, rather than steal.[9] In some cases, men would steal to provide for women, but the women themselves were usually dependent on either husbands or lovers to furnish them with worldly goods.

Not only were women always involved in interpersonal, rather than economic or political crimes, but they also tended to be either the victim or accomplice, rather than the perpetrator of a crime. This again reflects the generally passive role of the female. In only six of the cases studied (less than 9 percent) were women accused of committing a violent crime, and in two of these cases, the women accused were cited as accomplices rather than perpetrators.[10] It was rather as victims of violent interpersonal crime such as wife beating, rape, and kidnapping that women most frequently entered the legal records. More than half the cases reviewed fall into these categories. By far the most common crimes against women were physical abuse and wife beating, followed in frequency by rape and kidnapping. These crimes were usually committed against lower-class women, both in the city and in rural areas.

The crimes reported to the alcaldes tended to involve the artisan and lower classes, and the racial heterogeneity of the city was reflected in the cases. Indians, blacks, mestizos, mulattoes, and poor whites appear as victims, assailants, defendants, and witnesses. In general, the victim was of the same or less socially prestigious racial group than the assailant, but there were exceptions to this pattern. A few cases of rape and seduction involved white men and black women (one Portuguese was accused of having an uncontrollable passion for black women[11]), and a mulatto man was also accused of attacking a white woman.[12] Although the very fact that charges were brought by black women or their husbands against white men points to some degree of legal recourse for all classes and races, the crimes also reflected the city's racial hierarchy, only occasionally violated by "audacious" and "insolent" crimes.[13]

Central to an understanding of women's role in power relations is the question of the relationship between criminal and victim. Who committed crimes against whom? In the case of crime involving women in colonial Buenos Aires, crime was usually committed by family, friends, acquaintances, or neighbors. Rarely was crime of any nature against women committed by a stranger. The localized nature of crime reflected the familiar perimeters of the feminine world. In addition, most crime against women was committed in the home, again suggesting a limited social milieu for women. Most reported crimes were committed by people of similar social backgrounds as the victims, a reflection of the lack of social mobility and the class boundaries women faced in colonial society.

In general, crimes against women fall into two categories: domestic disturbances and sexual offenses. The first category, which included beating, stabbing, and attempted homicide, was almost by definition composed of crime occurring within the family. In these crimes, the wife was usually a victim of her husband's anger, although women were also abused by kinsmen.[14] Male anger could be fired by unseemly conduct on the part of the woman, her failure to conform to the norms of expected female behavior, especially sexual conduct. Several cases also reflect male violence in protecting his rights over the female members of his family when there was no indication of misconduct.

Much family crime reflects the high level of personal violence and frustration that was a normal part of lower-class male life. Men of the marginal urban and rural sectors, subsistence farmers, unskilled laborers, peons, and ranch laborers, lived in a world they could little control. Armed with knives, they turned their frustrations with their economic and social roles to the nearest available victim, their wives who were in a socially sanctioned subordinate position.

Domestic crime was usually reported to the local magistrates by the female victims themselves.[15] Women, especially married women, who had been repeatedly abused by their male kin, eventually sought protection from the local justices. Frequently their charges carried the complaint that they were being abused by the very men whose duty it was to defend them. Here they expressed the idealized societal norm that a man's duty was to protect his female kin.

Occasionally, physical abuse of a married woman was reported by a male relative such as her brother or father.[16] Obviously, many women, no matter how badly treated, were afraid to seek legal redress against their husbands, for they feared that physical abuse to which they were being subjected would be exacerbated. Testimony in these cases suggests the high degree of physical abuse that was tolerated by some women, often over long periods of time.[17]

At times, unrelated outsiders, often neighbors, would intervene to report the crime even when the victim herself chose not to press charges. This was especially true in cases where the physical abuse of a woman approached attempted homicide.[18] Neighbors generally ignored wife beating, considering it to be within a man's prerogatives to control and punish his wife, but when the physical abuse of a woman became so blatant and extreme as to threaten her life, custom and public morality forced neighbors to step into domestic disturbances to protect the endangered woman.

Although physical abuse was reported, judges tended to be lenient when dealing with these cases. Much of their questioning was concerned with the character of the woman involved, for if there was any stain on her reputation, her husband's conduct, no matter how inhumane, was absolved. The right of a husband to discipline a wife suspected of unseemly conduct (*mala conducta*) applied to all men regardless of race or legal condition; a slave could beat his wife although she belonged to another master.[19] The court's insistence on the need to document a female victim's good conduct, and the corollary that any treatment was justified to correct an evil woman, was also applied to cases involving wife murder. A wife's misconduct was the universal defense, although when murder was involved, witnesses were questioned closely, and this defense could occasionally backfire.[20]

The second major group of offenses that victimized women, sexual offenses, including rape, kidnap, and haircutting, also tended to be committed by men from within the same social world as the victim. Sexual offenses were almost uniformly committed by men known to their victims, by neighbors, acquaintances, or kin, fictive and real. Although lust was frequently the motivating force, these crimes were not random crimes of passion, but crimes in which the victim was well chosen by the assailant. When the victim of violent sexual crime was a married woman, the violence directed against her was at times just one step in a personal dispute between the assailant and the woman's husband. Arguments between men that had started over land, personal insults (*palabras injuriosas*), and affronts to a man's honor escalated to involve the married woman. For example, after Bartolomé Bordela intervened in a fight involving Alexo Machado and ordered him out of his house, Machado, swearing that Bordela would be made to pay, returned and attempted to rape Bordela's wife.[21] A married woman was the perfect victim in these disputes, for she was the means by which an enemy could assail her husband's manliness.[22] A husband's responsibility was to protect and care for his wife, for through the sacrament of marriage she had become part of his own flesh. A husband who was too weak to defend his wife, and his family's honor, was unworthy and despicable, the very antithesis of the macho ideal.[23] These crimes suggest that, at times, the married woman was assaulted as much because she was an object of desire, as she was the means by which to attack her husband and his honor.

When married women were the victims of violent sexual crimes, the legal complaints were always initiated by their husbands.[24] This reflected both the legal position of the married woman (unless she were the plaintiff and her husband were the assailant, she could not appear in court without his permission) and the belief that as head of his household, any attack against a man's wife was inevitably an attack against him. It was the man whose honor had been jeopardized, and it was the man who sought legal redress. Even in the very act of reporting the crime to a local magistrate, however, the man publicly admitted his vulnerability, and the fact that he was too weak to seek his own retribution. This is, perhaps, the reason that so many of the sexual offenses reported to local magistrates were charges of "attempted rape," rather than rape.[25] Successful rape and kidnapping were seldom reported to the authorities as such because of the attendant shame involved, but cases of attempted rape often included testimony on previously committed rape and kidnapping that had gone unreported.

In cases of sexual assault of unmarried women, it is more difficult to decide whether the woman was victimized because of her relationship to one of two feuding males or because of uncontrolled sexual passion. Again, as in crime against married women, the assailant was always an acquaintance of the woman involved, someone she had known, even fleetingly, before the crime was committed. Those single women with male protectors—a father, brother, or brother-in-law—turned to these men to report the crime and press charges.[26] In the case of single women with male protectors, some were victimized to destroy a male kinsman's honor, but the victims of violent sexual crimes were most often unprotected single women. Underlying this pattern of violence was the reality of a strongly male-dominated society that viewed unprotected females as fair game for sexual advances. Women, even temporarily, without husband, father, or brothers, were viewed as unprotected property, waiting to be claimed through male sexual prowess. For example, María Lino Cufré and María de la Concepción Masías, two women living alone in the city, were raped by two men who broke into their home at eleven o'clock one evening.[27]

In the countryside, women alone were even more frequent victims of rape and violence than in the city. Here, both married and single women, alone in their ranchos while their male kinsmen worked on the range, were attacked by men described as "guapos" or "gauderíos," men without obligations, precursors of the nineteenth-century gauchos.[28] Once a woman was sexually attacked, her violator often felt free to return and reclaim her whenever he pleased.[29]

Testimony from many of the cases suggests that among the more marginal social sectors, especially those living in the rural jurisdiction of the city, kidnapping and rape of unmarried girls were part of the local courtship pattern. After meeting an eligible young woman, a man would steal her from her home, usually at night or when the girl's male relatives were absent. Riding some distance from the "bride's" family, the girl was deflowered and the marriage thereby consummated without benefit of clergy. The couple then set up household, publicly living as man and wife. Only when the girl's family disapproved of her suitor, or when her new husband continued to "court" other women in the same way as he had wooed her, was any formal complaint lodged.[30]

In the absence of a male relative, single women brought rape and kidnapping charges against their assailants, either by themselves or through a female relative who acted on their behalf.[31] Single women had almost the same access to the legal system as did men, but they always underwent harsh grilling before their testimony was accepted by the magistrates. Even when charges were substantiated the rape or kidnapping of an unprotected single woman was often unpunished. Only the rape of a married woman was treated by the judges as a serious crime, for these crimes involved damage to a husband's honor. In all cases involving single women, the burden of proof was placed on the victim, and punishment was rarely meted out to the offender. Punishment was more likely to be exacted in those cases where a woman had a male guardian, husband, brother, or father, helping her in court. Again, criminals were punished more to assuage the masculine sense of honor and shame than to repay a woman for harm done her.

Even when sexual offenders were successfully prosecuted and punished, punishment tended to be lenient. The most frequent sentence for rape or forcible kidnapping was temporary exile to one of the towns on the other side of the La Plata estuary. Occasionally a criminal was sentenced to a longer period of exile—from one to ten years—in Colonia, Montevideo, or Santo Domingo Soriano, but there is little suggestion that life was harder in these towns than in the rural district of Buenos Aires. Exiled criminals were not closely guarded, and convicts frequently returned to Buenos Aires, only to be later accused of another crime.[32] Corporal punishment, consisting of twenty to two hundred lashes, was rare and was usually reserved for men who had raped young girls, or for slaves.[33]

The same attitude toward sexual attack on unprotected single women was present when female slaves were the victims of sexual assault, but here the crime was complicated by the fact that female slaves were also property. The slaves were, by their very condition, open to sexual abuse, but, surprisingly, some of them did initiate legal action on their own behalf, even at times against the wishes of their owners. In addition, female owners sometimes joined with their female slaves to complain of rape or sexual abuse of the latter.

The only cases of rape that greatly upset the local magistrates were those of child rape, cases in which the victim was less than fifteen years old. Even here, though, as in all cases of rape of an unmarried woman, the burden of proof was on the female, and complete physical entry had to be proved before the charges were felt to merit serious punishment.[34] Moreover when child rape was proved, the local judges tended to be more lenient than the law provided.[35] Leniency was also shown in a case involving a man guilty of "the most enormous and atrocious crime," having sexual relations with his wife's two adolescent daughters.[36] The criminal was sentenced to 150 lashes, a milder punishment than the death penalty, which the court pronounced for a young man accused of raping a male victim.[37] This punishment is the harshest sentence recorded for any sexual offense. Sodomy, unlike the rape of female children or women, was abhorrent, unnatural, contrary to God's law, and, therefore, warranted the most severe punishment.

Haircutting, although of lesser violence than rape or kidnapping, also had sexual significance. Cutting a woman's hair was tantamount to publicly branding a woman as morally loose. Jealousy or rejection was often the motive behind this crime, but again women were also slandered in this way in order to attack the honor of their male kinsmen. Antonio Pando went to court to bring charges against a neighbor who had cut his daughter's hair, for as a father, he was "more interested than anyone in the honor of my family."[38]

In almost all cases of crime against single women, the female victim was usually presumed both by the court and the social norms to have deserved the injury. If a woman invited a man into her house, even in broad daylight, rape was justified, as it was if a woman failed to lock her door at night or had shown any form of friendship to her assailant.[39] Women alone, whether for short or long periods of time, were also presumed to be inviting sexual abuse.[40] The same presumption that women deserved what befell them is also found in cases of physical abuse.

Because the courts, society, and their husbands could and did see the woman as deserving of the crime, some women, especially those of higher social standing, brought slander charges against neighbors and kinsmen who even suggested that their conduct was in any way less than proper.[41] The social code called for women to be pure, protected, and beyond reproach, and any indication that a woman failed to fulfill these norms presented great danger to her honor, that of her husband, and that of her family.

Although the social idea was a pure woman, almost half the cases reviewed involved women as accomplices in sexual misconduct—adultery and licentiousness. If the woman involved in the action was married, which she frequently was, her husband viewed himself as the public victim of her bad conduct. Charges were filed by the woman's offended husband, a local priest, or a morally indignant neighbor. Although the Laws of Toro (1505) required that both adulterers be charged and punished, usually only the man was formally accused. In those cases where the woman was formally charged with adultery, she was neither imprisoned during the trial, placed in *depósito*, nor sentenced after the verdict had been reached. Instead, she was returned to the care of her husband. Implicit in this attitude and in much of the testimony was the belief that women were, by their very nature, disorderly, prone to sexual excesses, and irrational in their sexual behavior. Regardless of the woman's cooperation in forming the adulterous union, the tempestuous female was not as guilty as her lover; rather the crime of adultery was perceived by society as being committed by one man against another man's wife.

There is no way to know how many women involved in adulterous unions were passive victims (single women or widows forced by economic pressures into sexual relations with married men), but some of the testimony suggests that there were women who took active roles in forming and perpetuating "illicit friendships," renewing them even after legal sanctions had been taken against the offending male, fleeing from their husbands to be with their lovers. María Pallero, wife of Matías Benites, fled twice—once from the home of a local priest where her husband had placed her for safekeeping—to join her lover.[42] María Antonia Florencia, wife of

Juan José Fredes, "known in all of the district where she lives and even farther away as a strumpet because of her impudence and fickleness," deserted her husband at least three times to live with three different men.[43] Such testimony suggests that women were involved in sexual relations of their own volition and reflects a degree of sexual freedom for the women of lower social groups within colonial society.

Court records also show that among the urban and rural poor, adultery was widely tolerated for long periods of time. Several cases contain testimony on adulterous unions that had been going on for as long as twenty years and were public knowledge.[44] Adultery was also tolerated by husbands who, although aware that they were being cuckolded, were either ashamed or afraid to file charges with the local judge.[45] The high incidence of illegitimate births attests to the widespread acceptance of illicit unions of both a casual and long-lasting sort. Adultery was not only generally ignored, but, much to the despair of civil and church authorities, couples often refused to obey repeated warnings to stop. Even imprisonment, which rarely lasted more than three months, did little to deter determined couples.[46]

Buenos Aires justice, and by extension Buenos Aires society, might have been lax in reprimanding adultery among the poor, but those groups with pretensions to higher social status were most vigilant in preventing their women from involvement in such sinful liaisons. Adulterous relationships involving *gente decente* ("decent people") are totally absent from the municipal court records, for in colonial *porteño* society, there was a fundamental conflict between honor and legality. For a man of the upper or middle class to appeal to municipal authorities to redress the wrong done to his honor by an adulterous wife was to demonstrate his vulnerability and to place his honor in even greater jeopardy. This did not mean that the guilty wife got off scot-free; instead adultery among the upper and middle class was viewed as a personal matter, and the sinning wife was packed off to either the local House of Religious Retreat or the Girls' Orphanage until she mended her ways.[47] All testimony points to the ease with which upper- and middle-class men could use extralegal mechanisms to send their wayward wives or daughters to these houses of correction or place them under the care of outstanding churchmen. This form of punishment maintained adultery as a private crime; only rarely did adultery among the *gente decente* become public knowledge through legal suits or divorce proceedings.[48]

According to Spanish law, a man was within his rights to murder a wayward wife and her lover, but among the more respectable classes of society, this was never done.[49] Again, such an action would have endangered a husband's honor by publicly manifesting his wife's betrayal. At times, though, adultery did lead to homicide among the lower classes, and a husband's right to punish the offenders was always a successful defense.[50] Occasionally it was the husband who was the homicide victim, and here the law showed no mercy to the defendants.[51]

In addition to complaints involving adulterous unions, charges were frequently brought against single men for waywardness and evil lifestyle (*mala vida*). Included in these general charges were complaints of rowdiness, concubinage, lawlessness, and repeated instances of attempted kidnapping and rape. The plaintiff was usually not any specific victim, man or woman, but a group of neighbors who feared that they would be victimized next. In many cases, this group action protected a man's honor by providing a degree of anonymity. When the legitimate victim, because of fear, helplessness, poverty, or social sanctions, failed to press charges, neighbors would join with him to file legal complaints if the criminal's actions were viewed as sufficiently threatening to the community at large. Colonial justice, while tolerating a high degree of personal violence, was, nevertheless, on guard against the type of lawlessness that threatened to terrorize whole districts of the city or countryside.

Criminal-court proceedings provide a glimpse of women as actors and objects, involved in the social and, to a lesser degree, the economic life of the city. Only upper-class women were able to conform to the societal norm of living sheltered, protected lives. Most colonial women, slave and free, black, Indian, mulata, *morena*, and even poor white, were forced by economic necessity to work in both urban and rural settings. These women were to be found on the ranchos of the countryside, in the rooms and *casitas* of the city, and in the homes of prominent local citizens. As *dependientes*, slaves, *agregadas*, day laborers; as single, married, or widowed women, they occupied a socially tenuous position, for the economic circumstances that forced them to work also exposed them to male violence, visited upon them by men of the same social class. In colonial society, women who were forced to defy the female norm of the protected, cloistered woman left themselves vulnerable to male abuse.

Frequent reference in criminal proceedings to unreported crime reflects one of the major problems of the colonial system of justice—its inaccessibility to large segments of the population. Especially in rural areas, generally isolated from even the officers of the Santa Hermandad, victims of crime had little recourse to justice. Reporting a crime entailed travel, time, money, and great determination. Once a crime was reported, the criminal had to be apprehended (not always an easy matter), witnesses found, and a judge and notary present to continue legal proceedings. Often defendants, victims, and witnesses were forced to travel to Buenos Aires for the trial.

Testimony from criminal trials reveals only a small percentage of actual crime, but it does present a picture of the types of crimes women participated in or were victimized by, as well as reflecting the dominant male culture of colonial Hispanic society. There were definite inconsistencies in that culture's view of women. Women were expected to be pure, docile, obedient, and churchgoing. Beneath the surface, however, women were believed to be sensual, lascivious creatures, in constant need of protection, guidance, discipline, and punishment. A husband's legal duty was to provide sustenance and shelter for his wife. She in return was bound to obey him, show him respect, protect his honor, and submit to his discipline. A man publicly stating that "he felt like fighting and punishing a woman" was hardly viewed as unusual.[52] Especially among the lower classes, women were viewed as natural outlets for male aggression.

Colonial society displayed a high level of personal violence, especially among the lower classes and more rural elements. Frequently, crime against women, especially violent sexual crime, served as a surrogate, an effective way of impugning a man's honor by damaging his property and emphasizing his inability to defend his woman in a "manly" manner. The weak in this society were triply victimized—by those who attacked their honor, by the frustrations involved in appealing to local justice, and by the general lack of retribution this justice, once activated, provided.

Notes

The author wishes to thank the National Endowment for the Humanities whose support made this research possible. This essay originally appeared in *Journal of Latin American Studies* (May 1980): 39-54, and is reprinted by permission.

1. Crime in France has been studied by Yves Castan, Porphyre Petrovitch, and Nicole Castan among others; their essays appear in A. Abbiateci et al., *Crimes et criminalité en France sous l'Ancien Régime: 17e-18e siècles* (Paris, 1971). See also Louis Chevalier, *Laboring Classes and Dangerous Classes in Paris during the First Half of the Nineteenth Century* (New York, 1973). Historians of crime in pre-nineteenth-century England include J. S. Cockburn, J. A. Sharpe, Joel Samaha, Douglas Hay, and J. M. Beattie. See J. S. Cockburn, ed., *Crime in England, 1550–1800* (Princeton, 1977) for an excellent annotated bibliography. In addition, the entire issue of the *Journal of Social History* (Summer, 1975); is devoted to studies in the history of crime in Europe.

2. Among the few studies in Latin American history dealing with crime are Colin MacLachlan, *Criminal Justice in Eighteenth Century Mexico: A Study of the Tribunal of the Acordada* (Berkeley, 1974) and Patricia Ann Aufderheide, "Order and Violence: Social Deviance and Social Control in Brazil, 1780–1840," Ph.D. dissertation, University of Minnesota, 1976.

3. Carol Z. Wiener, "Sex-Roles and Crime in Late Elizabethan Hertfordshire," *Journal of Social History* (Summer 1975): 38.

4. For a theoretical discussion of the law as it applied to women, see José María Ots Capdequí, "Bosquejo histórico de los derechos de la mujer en la legislación de Indias," *Revista General de Legislación y Jurisprudencia* (Colegio de Abogados, Madrid) (July-December 1934): 185–206, 324–39; (January-March 1935): 162–82; (April-June 1935): 5-33; 222–38; (October-December 1935): 141–55; (January-March 1936): 43–55, 411–25, 498–514; (April-June 1936): 139–53, 339–62.

5. These cases are found in the Archivo General de la Nación Argentina, Buenos Aires (hereinafter AGNA), Criminales, and in the Archivo de la Provincia de Buenos Aires, La Plata (hereinafter APBA), Criminales.

6. For an idea of the variety of female roles and occupations, see Padrón de la ciudad de Buenos Aires, 1744, in Facultad de Filosofía y Letras, *Documentos para la historia argentina*, Tomo X, *Padrones* (Buenos Aires, 1920), pp. 329–502. Similar evidence for relatively large numbers of working

women has been found in at least one city of Colonial Brazil. See Donald Ramos, "Marriage and Family in Colonial Vila Rica," *Hispanic American Historical Review* (May 1975): 221–22.

7. For an example of research based on ecclesiastical records, see Silvia M. Arrom, *La mujer mexicana ante el divorcio eclesiástico (1800–1857)* (Mexico City, 1976).

8. Weiner, "Sex-Roles and Crime," 40.

9. The economic reasons for entering into an illicit relationship are seen in APBA, Criminales, 1789, 34–1–15, Causa criminal seguida de oficio contra Juan Porta o Puente por amancebamiento con María Magdalena Aguilar.

10. Cases with women assailants include AGNA, Criminales, 1761, leg. 3, exp. 7, IX–31–1–0, Proceso criminal contra Dominga negra esclava de don Juan Lopez Camelo (summarized in Marcelo Bazán Lazcano, "Inventario analítico de la serie criminales (1756–1810)," *Revista del Archivo General de la Nación* (1974): 320–23; AGNA, Criminales, leg. 4, exp. 13, IX–32–1–1, Proceso criminal contra Francisco González y otros (Bazán, 344–45); AGNA, Criminales, leg. 1, exp. 6, IX–31–9–7, 1757, Proceso criminal contra Victor Pavón, Juan José Acosta y Gerónima india por homicidio (Bazán, 289–91).

11. APBA, Criminales, 1778, 34–1–9, Querella dada por Miguel Rodrigues de la Rosa contra Manuel Gonzales de Silba por procurar este tener ilícita amistad con la mujer de aquel.

12. APBA, Criminales, 1796, 34–1–21, Pedro Losano contra José Antonio Mansilla mulato por haver golpeado a una mujer casada y luego forzarla.

13. APBA, Criminales, 1796, 34–1–21, Pedro Losano contra José Antonio Mansilla.

14. APBA, Criminales, 1793, 34–1–18, Narcisca Cordero contra su yerno Calisto Baigorria por haverla pegado.

15. For example, see APBA, Criminales, 1785–86, 34–1–13, María del Carmen Troncoso contra su esposo don Juan Tomás Luzano por injuria.

16. APBA, Criminales, 1796, 34–1–21, Querella criminal puesta por Naciso Rodríguez contra José Gregorio Gaytán por los injurias que causó este a la mujer de Rodríguez y a una hija suya casada.

17. APBA, Criminales, 1783–84, 34–1–12, María Antonia Josefa de Aguilar sobre los malos tratamientos de su marido Simón Launar.

18. APBA, Criminales, 1790–91, 34–1–16, Contra Santiago Gaeta por intentar quitar la vida a su esposa.

19. APBA, Criminales, 1789, 34–1–15, Contra el mulato Manuel Malaves por haber herido a su mujer María Isabel Orbe.

20. AGNA, Criminales, leg. 7, exp. 19, IX–32–1–4, 1773, Causa criminal contra Hermenegildo Tabacaque, indio (Bazán, 399–402).

21. APBA, Criminales, 1790, 34–1–16, Bartolomé Bordela contra Alexo Machado por haver tratado ilicitamente con violenta fuerza con su esposa.

22. Aufderheide, "Order and Violence," pp. 168, 171.

23. Julian Pitt-Rivers, "Honour and Social Status," in J. C. Peristiany, ed., *Honor and Shame: The Values of Mediterranean Society* (Chicago, 1966), p. 30.

24. APBA, Criminales, 1795, 32–1–20, Gregorio Vejarano contra Pedro Correa por haver forzado a la mujer y hija de aquello.

25. APBA, Criminales, 1790, 32–1–16, Alonso Domingo contra Félix Fernández por haver violado y querido forzar a su mujer.

26. APBA, Criminales, 1781–82, 34–1–11, Autos criminales contra Juan Rosales por varios excesos.

27. APBA, Criminales, 1779–80, 34–1–10, Autos criminales seguidos por la Real Justicia contra Gerónimo Miranda y Sebastián Brito sobre la violencia que han hecho a María Lino y María de la Concepción.

28. APBA, Criminales, 1780, 34–1–10, Causa criminal contra Ignacio Urreta por ilícita amistad con una mujer casada; APBA, 1795, 34–1–20, Gregorio Vejarona contra Pedro Correa por haver forzado a la mujer hija de aquello; APBA, Criminales 1797, 34–1–22, Sumaria obrada por el Teniente del cuerpo de Blandenguez de la Frontera de Buenos Aires don Antonio González.

29. APBA, Criminales, 1780, 34–1–10, Causa criminal contra Ignacio Urreta.

30. APBA, Criminales, 1785–86, 34–1–13, Autos criminales seguidos por la Real Justicia contra Miguel Godoy por haberse querido robar una niña de poder de su madre y después de casa de su cura don Luis de Tagle que lo es de la capilla del Pilar; APBA, Criminales, 1785, 34–1–13, Sumaria contra Basilio Bustamante y María de los Santos por amancebados.

31. APBA, Criminales, 1797, 34–1–22, Contra Plácido Díaz por haver violado a una niña.

32. APBA, Criminales, 1781–82, 34–1–11, Sumaria obrada contra Pedro Calzada por el Alcalde de la Santa Hermandad don Isidro Fernández.

33. The idea of harsher treatment for slaves was not new to Spanish jurisprudence. The Fuero Juzgo, lib. 3, tít. 4, l. 14, sets the punishment for a free man who forces a woman into adultery at one hundred lashes, while a slave is to be burnt at the stake for the same crime.

34. APBA, Criminales, 1793, 34–1–18, Contra Miguel Sánchez por quererla forzar violentamente a la hija de Braviela Toledo.

35. APBA, Criminales, 1776–78, 34–1–9, Autos que de oficio se siguen contra Dionicio Salazar pardo esclavo de don Francisco Congett Cordovez

por haver comitido delito de estrupro en una muchacha de edad de siete o ocho años.

36. AGNA, Criminales, 1783–84, 34–1–12, Contra Domingo Cazquero por haver tenido cópula carnal con dos hijas de su mujer María Bernanda Escobar.

37. AGNA, Criminales, leg. 7, exp. 9, IX–32–1–4, 1772, Autos criminales contra Mariano de los Santos Toledo por sodomía (Bazán, 381–90).

38. APBA, Criminales, 1794, 34–1–19, Causa criminal seguida contra Juan Rodríguez por Antonio Pando. See another mention of haircutting in C. R. Boxer, *Women in Iberian Expansion Overseas, 1415–1815: Some Facts, Fancies and Personalities* (New York, 1975), Appendix II, pp. 115–16.

39. APBA, Criminales, 1779–80, 34–1–10, Autos criminales seguidos por la Real Justicia contra Gerónimo Mirando y Sebastián Brito.

40. APBA, Criminales, 1790–91, 34–1–16, Contra Alexo Machado; and APBA, Criminales, 1797, 34–1–22, Contra Plácido Díaz por haver violado a una niña.

41. APBA, Criminales, 1797, 34–1–22, Querella criminal puesta por María Petrona Fernández contra Manuel Mallorca por haverla injuriada de malas palabras.

42. APBA, Criminales, 1785, 34–1–13, Autos criminales contra Paulino Troncoso por amancevamiento con una mujer casada.

43. APBA, Criminales, 1793, 34–1–18, Juan Josef Fredes contra su mujer María Antonia Florencia y Gaspar Calderón.

44. APBA, Criminales, 1789, 34–1–15, Criminales a pedimento de Juan Martínez contra su mujer Manuela Raya y Félix Alberto por adultero.

45. APBA, Criminales, 1778, 34–1–9, Causa criminal contra María Magdalena Moreira y Manuel Iriarte por haver cometido con él dicha adulterio.

46. APBA, Criminales, 1795, 34–1–20, Félix Rivera contra Clemente Reinosa y Margarita Toledo por ilícita amistad.

47. AGNA, Hermandad de la Caridad, Acuerdos, leg. 6, IX–6–8–5.

48. For the few cases of divorce proceedings in which adultery is mentioned, see Pedro Grenon, "Nuestros divorcios históricos," *Historia* (1958): 5–19. Unfortunately, the records on which this article was based have been destroyed.

49. For the source of this law, see Fuero Juzgo, lib. 3, tít 4, l. 4.

50. AGNA, Criminales, leg. 2, exp. 4, IX–31–9–8, 1759, Causa criminal contra Clemente Garrucho o Viyazare y otros (Bazán, 297–98).

51. AGNA, Criminales, leg. 7, exp. 12, IX–32–1–4, 1770, Causa criminal contra Antonio Espinoza, peón de a caballo y Paula Torres (Bazán, 391–94).

52. APBA, Criminales, 1790–91, 34-1-16, Bartolomé Bordela contra Alexo Machado.

2

Continuities in Crime and Punishment

Buenos Aires, 1820–50

Richard W. Slatta and Karla Robinson

In Argentina's polemical, politicized historiography, sharp distinctions have been drawn between the centralist rule of Bernadino Rivadavia and the Unitarios during the 1820s and the subsequent dictatorship of Juan Manuel de Rosas. The nation's liberal historians paint the transition as one from incipient democracy and economic and cultural advancement to a dark age of isolationism, repression, and "barbarism." Revisionist partisans of Rosas transform the villains into heroes. They portray Rosas as the heroic defender of the nation who saved Argentina from the *vendipatria* policies of the Unitarios. Both positions stress the great differences between these two periods.[1]

Records of the criminal-justice system for the city and province of Buenos Aires, however, reveal overarching continuities between the Unitario and Rosista periods. Similar types of crimes were committed, and analogous, sometimes arbitrary, punishments were meted out. During the first several decades of national life, Unitario and Rosista officials determined to impose an often-harsh social control over the masses.

Rosas was more an oppressor than a champion of the masses. Far from repudiating the class attitudes that demanded attacks on the rural and urban masses, Rosas vigorously enforced and even broadened social-control legislation originated by Bernadino Rivadavia. The *gente decente* ("decent people"), Unitario or Rosista, seeking to preserve their economic interests and social position, increased and extended formal legal mechanisms to promote their class interests and safety. This mobilization of law enforcement on behalf of elites follows similar patterns detected in the cities of Calcutta, London, Stockholm, and Sydney.[2]

National and provincial political conflict, coupled with rapid pop-

ulation growth and economic expansion, made Buenos Aires a tur-
bulent city during the 1830s and 1840s. The city, affectionately
termed the Gran Aldea by its inhabitants, enjoyed growth and vital-
ity, but it also suffered from multiplying urban problems. By the
1820s, it was one of South America's largest cities and extended
for about two miles from north to south and about one-half mile
from east to west. The number of houses, often dilapidated, white
stuccoed with green wrought-iron gratings, may have run to six
thousand at the beginning of the 1820s. Population estimates ranged
from 55,416 in 1822 to 81,000 in 1824, with the actual total probably nearer the lower figure. In 1822, about 63,230 people inhab-
ited the countryside surrounding the city. An incomplete census
in 1836 recorded 62,228 city dwellers and another 80,729 people in
the counties nearby. Better figures, although still based on incomplete census returns, give for 1854–55 totals of 90,076 in the city
and 183,861 in the countryside. Using the 1822 and 1854–55 figures, we find that the city grew at an annual rate of 1.9 percent
and the countryside at a much higher rate of 5.8 percent. The big
village was becoming a city, with all the resulting problems.[3]

Contraband trade, especially of silver, slaves, and hides, flour-
ished during the colonial era, and the evasion of customs and out-
right theft continued thereafter. Well into the nineteenth century,
a system of black-market capitalism moved stolen hides from gauchos and Indians to porteño merchants and then to European markets. Arriving at the port in 1819, an English visitor observed that
drivers of the carts "manifest great intelligence and adroitness,
joined to no small portion of knavery; for such articles as can be
easily purloined commonly disappear in the transit from the craft
to the shore."[4]

Among the city's many business establishments, the pulpería,
a combination general store and tavern, far outnumbered any other
type. The Blondell business almanac for 1826 listed some 464
pulperías. They usually occupied strategic street corners along most
thoroughfares and as a result were also called *esquinas*. These
cramped, primitive stores furnished a miscellany of general merchandise, foodstuffs, and liquor sold to slaves, who shopped for
their masters, and to lower-class patrons. Gamblers, inflamed with
the pulpero's ready supply of cheap but potent liquor, often dueled
with long swordlike knives called *facones*. Death or serious injury

frequently resulted. As a Scottish traveler observed, "Numberless are the crosses about the doors of the pulperías." Pulperías in both the city and the countryside served as theaters for many crimes of violence, generally attacks by one patron on another.[5]

Pulperías received special legal scrutiny because of their reputation for violence and lawlessness. Early in 1827, police arrested three men in the city for frequenting a pulpería during working hours. Two of the men had work contracts as required by law, but stood in violation of a statute against drinking at a tavern when they should have been working. The third had neither a work contract nor military enrollment certificate and thus became a suspected vagrant.[6] Military commanders seeking recruits for the army or frontier militia often swept the pulperías where at least some of the patrons could likely be found in violation of the law.

Violence in the pulperías and in the streets aroused fear among the residents of Buenos Aires. Since the colonial period, the *gente decente* had despised and feared the urban masses, who were thought to be unruly and criminal. These sharp class prejudices divided Porteño society even more than the issue of race. *El Argos* (Buenos Aires) of 7 July 1821 complained of governmental indifference to urban crime. The Porteño newspaper urged that the new governing junta create a police force adequate to the needs of a growing city the size of Buenos Aires. Rural vagrancy and thefts preoccupied authorities, according to the paper, to the seeming exclusion of urban crime problems. Indeed, Rivadavia had assigned new rural *comisarios* to promote "public tranquility" and stamp out illegal gambling in the countryside.

Organized protection came in 1821 with the creation of a municipal police department. Joaquín de Achaval headed the new department and charged his *peoneros de policía* with the particular duty of keeping a watchful eye on vagrants, widely believed to lounge about the city's numerous pulperías. Like officers in most early municipal forces, police in Buenos Aires had responsibility for a wide range of other duties, including the enforcement of health regulations in bakeries, the maintenance of clean streets open to transit, and the removal of dead animals from public places. By 1837, the municipal force numbered sixty mounted police and another forty-five patrolling on foot.[7]

The new police force diligently set about upholding the social order. A decree signed by Rivadavia on 11 June 1822 directed that anyone found drunk and lacking property and employment be classified a public vagrant and prosecuted accordingly. Property owners and employed persons found drunk in public were to be jailed for twenty-four hours. Subsequent arrests would carry longer jail terms of up to a month's time, and a fifth offense would precipitate a trial before a judge and more serious penalties. As the city and surrounding areas grew, and with it the multiplying problems of crime and social control, the government expanded and reorganized the police department. A new system created in 1825 divided the city into four police districts, each under the authority of a *comisario*.[8]

Nighttime proved particularly dangerous to porteños because of assaults and robberies committed under the cover of darkness. Achaval had urged that night patrols be instituted in 1821, but no action was taken at that time. In September 1833, Gen. Juan Ramón Balcarce ordered the establishment of night patrols throughout the city. Working with pistols, a lantern, and a warning whistle, night patrols tried to deter and apprehend nocturnal criminals. Before the organization of the police force, Porteños had taken turns at patrol duty or paid a substitute to serve. In 1834, the municipality resurrected this practice and assigned vigilante patrols of townsmen both day and night. Night patrols were cautioned to watch pulperías with special care and listen for obscene language in the streets. The law also obligated all citizens to render assistance to vigilante patrols if called upon and assist in the prevention of crimes and the detention of criminals.[9] Thus, the control of urban crime again became the responsibility not only of the police but also of society in general.

Who were the criminals that so troubled the residents, police, and politicians of Buenos Aires? Males accounted for 94.7 percent of the arrests and incarcerations examined. Within that male population, those aged twenty to thirty-nine accounted for nearly three-fourths of arrests and jailings. Boys aged seven to nineteen contributed another 12 percent. The youngest criminal recorded, seven-year-old Angel López, was jailed in late 1849 for stealing 505 pesos from doña Teresa Beraza. Males older than thirty-nine perpetrated only 14 percent of all crimes. Only for the crime of gambling did older men face conviction in substantial numbers. Men in their forties received sentences for gambling nearly twice as often as they did for any other major type of crime. They comprised 17.5 percent of arrested gamblers but only about 8 or 9 percent of other types of criminals.[10]

The young men committing crimes in Buenos Aires were usually unmarried. This circumstance does not readily distinguish them from the general population, because most young men, particularly those from rural areas, found few opportunities for marriage and stable family life. Single men committed 62 percent of the crimes attributed to men, while married men committed 36 percent and widowers 3 percent. Although directly comparable figures are not readily available, these proportions likely parallel the civil statuses for men in the population at large. Only for the crime of gambling did married men break the law as often as single men. Both groups accounted for 48 percent of gambling convictions. Higher rates of marriage correspond with older age, so that the men in their forties convicted of gambling were also more likely to be married than younger men.

Since colonial times, authorities had worried over the preponderance of young, unmarried males in the population. "Footloose and fancy free," these young men were thought to be prone to violence and perhaps to dangerous political activity. In the Río de la Plata, bachelors, to the official eye, appeared too mobile, prone to illegal activity, and indifferent to civic responsibilities.[11]

The powerful cultural force of machismo also created a model of men as intemperate, obstinate, and ruled by violent passions. Women, according to their culturally assigned role of *marianismo*, were to be pure, spiritual, domestic, and pacific and thereby serve as sources of ballast and morality to moderate the excesses of males. Officials wished for responsible married men with a stake in the stability and well-being of society. They feared unattached, migratory types, such as migrants from the interior provinces and gauchos who seemed to roam, drink, gamble, and fight too much.[12]

Prosecution of suspected vagrants coupled with the migratory, seasonal nature of ranch employment made it unlikely if not impossible for rural males to settle down to a stable lifestyle. High levels of migration from the interior to the littoral, especially among male workers, also meant that many *provincianos* left their families elsewhere. This weighted the sex ratio toward males in the littoral. In addition, the concentration of land ownership prevented much of the rural population from settling permanently on the land. The omnipresent threat of forced military service deterred many rural workers from living anywhere for very long, even when such a rare opportunity presented itself.[13] Thus it is not surprising to find young single men prominently represented in the criminal population in both the city and countryside.

In contrast to men, married women and widows were arrested for more crimes than single women. Each of the two former groups accounted for 39 percent of female arrests (78 percent total), while single women contributed only 22 percent. The small number of cases involved (76 women total) mandates caution in generalizing about women and criminal behavior. These figures, though, probably reflect the civil status for women in the general population. Always in short supply vis-à-vis males, marriageable women usually wed early and survived their husbands. It was not unusual to find widows in charge of large estancias in Buenos Aires province. With regard to age and civil status, neither arrested males nor females deviated greatly from the population at large.[14]

If age and civil status show no striking patterns among the criminal population, occupation clearly does. During the nineteenth century, officials worried about rural males who supported rebellious caudillos. Motivated far less by political ideology than by promises of booty, pillage, and adventure, such forces constituted a dangerous military and political threat to established elites. Under these circumstances, it is not surprising that the heaviest measure of criminal and social control fell upon rural society. Urban crimes, while abhorrent to porteño officials, did not represent as potent a social and political danger as did ranch workers turned cavalrymen. Of the persons in jail in 1822, 40 percent were rural workers, and more than three-fourths of them labored at equestrian jobs (ranch peons, guides, hunters, and carters). These gaucho types were greatly overrepresented in the arrested population. Of the 118,646 persons in the county and city of Buenos Aires in 1822, only about 15,808 (14 percent) were gauchos. Thus, the proportion of their arrests stood at nearly three times the proportion in the population at large.[15]

Were rural males more violent and lawless than other sectors of society? The answer must be yes; they lived in a violence-prone, macho subculture on the frontier. They also suffered, though, from legal constraints not applied to city dwellers. Officials termed landless rural males "gauchos," a term that assumed lower-class birth and criminality. Gradually the term came to refer to any male who did mounted, especially ranch, labor. The Porteño elite aimed passports, military-enrollment forms, working papers, and some vagrancy laws at the rural population. Some major categories of crime applied mainly to rural workers (notably that of *vago y mal entretenido*). A common gaucho response to these attempts at social control was to ignore or resist the laws. As a result, the rural landless masses were disproportionately present in the criminal population and came to be viewed with alarm and distrust by Argentine officials and elites, much like Europeans and North Americans viewed their "dangerous classes."[16]

Urban laborers and artisans comprised the second largest occupational class of persons arrested, accounting for 31 percent. Taken together, the rural and urban working classes were arrested for 71 percent of all crimes. The urban propertied and professional groups were not totally absent. They committed about 8 percent of all crimes. Table 1 and Figure 1 provide a summary of criminal activity by occupation. The much feared "unemployed and vagrant" population, targeted by a plethora of restrictive legislation, represented only a tiny fraction (4 percent) of convicted criminals. The legal constraints putatively directed against vagrants were rather designed to coerce and control the seasonally employed and highly mobile rural population and maintain the established social order.[17]

The porteño elite also perceived slaves as a potentially danger-

Table 1

Occupations of Prisoners in Buenos Aires, City and Province, 1822

Occupation	Number	Percent of total
Rural Workers	276	40
Urban Workers	216	31
Maritime	61	9
Urban Propertied and Professional	53	8
Slaves	47	7
Unemployed or Vagrant	29	4
Soldiers	6	1
Totals:	688	100

Source: Sample 1.

Figure 1
Occupations of Prisoners in Buenos Aires,
City and Province, 1822

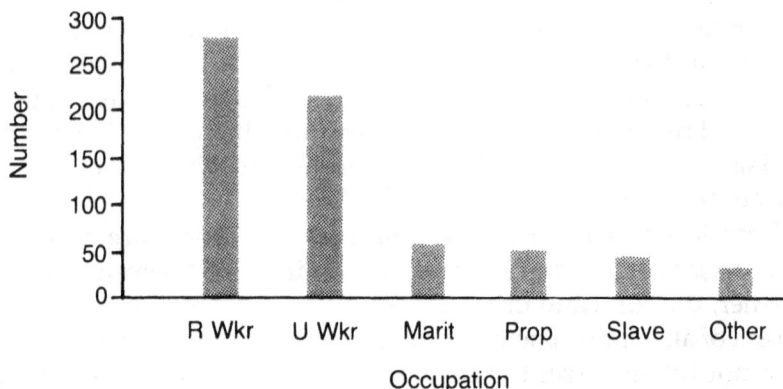

Key to Occupations

Rural Workers
Urban Workers
Maritime Workers
Propertied and Professional
Slaves
Others (Soldiers, Unemployed, Vagrant)

Source: Sample 1.

ous social group. Slavery persisted under a number of guises in Buenos Aires until its definitive abolition in 1862. Reid Andrews has detailed the devious mechanisms and loopholes slave holders, including Rosas, used to maintain their property long after 1813, when several laws limited the institution. For example, in 1831, police officials mysteriously lost registers containing evidence that would have freed some *libertos*, slave offspring who should have been freed at maturity or marriage. Because of hidden servitude, the proportion of truly free and enslaved blacks in Buenos Aires remains unclear. It appears, however, that slaves were slightly underrepresented in the criminal population. Slaves accounted for only 9 percent of incarcerations compared with 91 percent for free persons jailed in 1822. Officially, slaves represented 12 percent of the city's population (6,611 of 55,416 people) in 1822. Slave holders most often filed charges against their slaves for running away, stealing, or physically attacking them or their overseers. In June 1831, María Liberta (a black woman) charged her slave, Luis Gelpes, with striking her. That same month, a slave named Juana Leocadia was charged with knifing Antonia Giménez.[18]

Even noncriminal slaves came under extraordinary demands because of their servile legal condition. In 1826, Bernadino Rivadavia ordered police to compile lists of all Porteño slaves suitable for military service. The lists were to be turned over to the Ministro de Marina y Guerra so that slaves could supplement the criminals, draftees, and few volunteers that made up the Argentine military forces. Another decree of May 1826 placed free Blacks under jeopardy as well. Police conscripted 5 blacks per cuartel into military service (a total of 215 men).[19]

As is the proportion of slave to free, the true racial composition of Buenos Aires is difficult to measure. An official count of the city in 1822 revealed the following: 73 percent white, 25 percent Afro-Argentine, and 2 percent mestizo or Indian. A census five years later gave 80 percent white, 19.6 percent Afro-Argentine, and a fraction of a percent of mestizos and Indians. These figures apparently count trigueños ("wheat-colored") as whites, thereby distorting the true racial composition. Table 2 and Figure 2 provide a racial distribution of offenders for the year 1822. Correcting for the trigueño-white proportions, these criminal statistics closely mirror the racial composition of Buenos Aires given in the official census of 1822. The 21 percent listed as trigueño included dark-skinned persons of many racial mixtures and even swarthy Europeans. Likewise, the term pardo referred to persons of mixed blood regardless of the specific components. Moreno denoted persons of pure African descent.[20] Race per se does not appear to be a significant element in determining who was jailed in 1822.

Like the migratory rural population, the blacks of Buenos Aires were singled out for special social-control legislation. Seeking to enforce strict control over Afro-Argentines, free and slave, officials resurrected colonial decrees against black dancing in the streets (candombés). In February 1822, Rivadavia decreed that all blacks found dancing in the streets would be assigned to labor on public-

Table 2
Race* of Prisoners in Buenos Aires, City and Province, 1822

Race	Number	Percent of Total
White	412	53
Trigueño	165	21
Moreno	112	14
Pardo	69	9
Indian	17	2
Sambo	1	0.1
Totals:	776	99.1(rounding error)

*Race is the term employed in the documents. It is recognized that these terms are not technically racial categories, but delineations of color and ethnicity.
Source: Sample 1.

Figure 2
Race of Prisoners in Buenos Aires,
City and Province, 1822

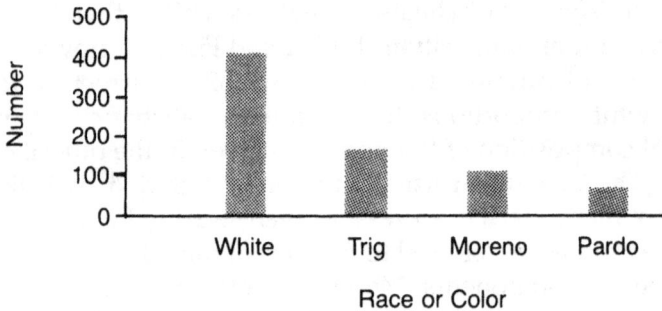

Key to Races

White
Trigueño
Moreno
Pardo
(Indian and Sambo omitted: total = 2.1%)

Source: Sample 1.

works projects for one month. He repeated the ban on *candombé* the following year. An order signed 21 June 1825 by Manuel García again prohibited *candombé* as an offense to public morality. Presidents of black societies, however, could petition for special permission to perform such dances. In one of his few deviations from Unitario law enforcement, Rosas ended the ban on *candombés* and even attended performances personally. By this and other demagogic acts, Rosas strengthened popular support for his leadership among porteño blacks.[21]

Given the cultural machismo of early nineteenth-century Argentina, it is not surprising to find women were a very small minority in the criminal-justice system, just as they remained nearly invisible in other areas of public life. Rigid cultural norms relegated women to the *casa* and left public affairs of the *calle* to men. Women played varied and vital economic roles throughout the colonial era and into the national period, but the economic contributions of women did not translate into social and legal equality. Adult women, whether married or single, retained the legal status of minors.[22]

Legal inequities, coupled with powerful social norms, shaped the position of women in the Argentine criminal justice system. Current criminological research shows that police often ascribe characteristics to alleged criminals on the basis of gender. Police are predisposed to evaluate men and women very differently. On the one hand, in our sample of 1,462 criminal cases for which sex of the offender is known, women committed only 5.3 percent. On the other, women were victims in 25 percent of those crimes in which the sex of the victim is known, usually as the object of violent, personal attack.[23] Differences between the sexes emerge in the specific types of crimes committed.

What types of crimes did the many male and relatively few female offenders commit? Crimes perpetrated in Buenos Aires and the surrounding countryside ranged from violent physical attacks and murder to innocuous, victimless crimes of little importance or injury. Infractions have been categorized into five major types. Crimes against persons (39 percent) included violent assault, murder, fighting, rape, kidnapping, and other attacks on a person or persons by others. Crimes against property (32 percent) included all thefts, but also embezzlement, transport or sale of stolen goods, fraud, and other types of economic wrongdoing. Crimes against the social order (18 percent) were of particular concern to officials because of the potential political and social significance of such threats to the prevailing status system. Some of these crimes were perceived as dangerous because of their potentially subversive or even revolutionary character. Breaking curfew, vagrancy, public insults, disorder, drunkenness, and being "incorregible" or "suspicious" were among the charges that threatened the social order. The category of fugitive (5 percent) includes a variety of criminals who fled or otherwise evaded civil or military officials. The core of this group consists of army deserters and runaway slaves, but other escapees and fugitives from justice are also included. The vastness of the pampas, the sparseness of settlement, and the great mobility of well-mounted horsemen made fugitives a particularly vexing problem for provincial law-enforcement officials. Detailed physical descriptions of deserters and fugitives (*filiaciones*) circulated widely among provincial authorities. The final 6 percent of crimes came from gambling infractions, a favorite pastime of both rural and urban Argentines. A game of chance called *taba* and the *riña*, or cockfight, remained popular throughout the century. Sixty-five of the 79 arrests for gambling involved cockfights, and repeated prohibitions never successfully suppressed the spectacle.[24]

Examining the categories of crime individually, the attacks on persons add substantive evidence to the violent reputation of the Unitario and Rosas eras. Drunkenness and looting prevailed among military men, and with military might dictating the direction of provincial and national politics, it is consistent that violence also suffused cotidian life. Among prisoners held in 1822, rural workers committed 38 percent of the attacks on persons that were perpetrated by males, and urban workers contributed another 34 percent. Most of the relatively few personal attacks committed by women occurred in the countryside.[25]

Property crimes also show a disproportionate number of rural infractions. Rural workers committed 43 percent of all thefts and other crimes involving property. Many of these cases involved the theft or sale of stolen hides or wool. Such livestock losses, while minor in comparison with those resulting from natural disaster and disease, prompted ranchers to cry out repeatedly for measures against rustlers. Concern over livestock thefts led to some legislation banning or limiting the activities of itinerant peddlers (*pulperos volantes*) widely suspected of purchasing illicit goods and thereby encouraging rustling.

Urban workers committed 25 percent of thefts. Urban thefts generally involved relatively minor items. In early 1821, however, thieves broke into the cabildo and took stamped gold (leaving the silver) from the strongbox in the amount of 3,247 pesos; the town then purchased a much more serviceable one. It is difficult to assess whether the actual incidence of crime in the countryside (as opposed to the official record) was higher than for urban areas. Given official concern about rural disorder, the difference may be in enforcement and arrest rather than in the actual number of crimes committed.[26]

Infractions against the social order and for gambling were nearly equal in rural and urban areas. Given the greater population density and visibility of disturbances in Buenos Aires, Porteño police made more arrests for such crimes than did officials in the countryside. Table 3 and Figure 3 show the distribution of criminal acts by occupation for males.

Differences between the sexes in the types of crimes committed

Table 3
Occupational Distribution of Male Prisoners in Buenos Aires,
City and Province, 1822, by Type of Crime

Occupation	Property	Personal Attack	Social Order	Gambling	Fugitive	Total
Rural Worker	100	78	23	18	5	224
Urban Worker	59	70	22	20	10	181
Maritime	22	15	4	1	3	45
Slave	17	14	9	4	1	45
Urban Propertied and Professional	15	12	6	6	1	40
Unemployed	9	3	4	5	2	23
Total:	222	192	68	54	22	558

Source: Sample 1.

Figure 3
Number of Arrests by Type of Crime Committed
for Male Prisoners in Buenos Aires, City and Province, 1822

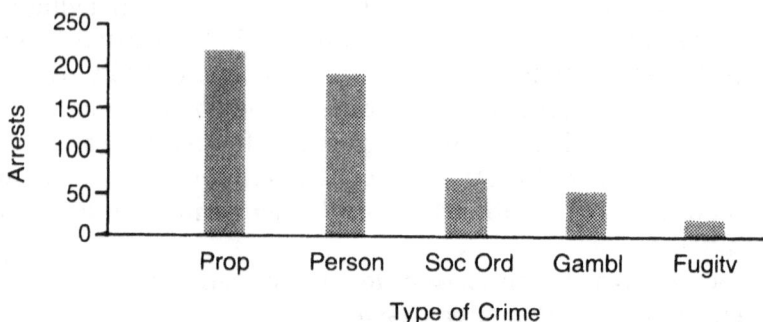

Key to Crimes

Crimes against Property
Crimes against Persons
Crimes against the Social Order
Gambling
Fugitives

Source: Sample 1.

emerged clearly from the data for the entire period. Crimes of violence against persons made up 38 percent of all male violations but only 21 percent of female infractions. Men, particularly rural men, carried knives most of the time and confronted one another in a violence-prone, macho world. Attacks by women most often occurred during family quarrels or against another woman. In the latter case, the resulting arrest would more often be considered a public disturbance or nuisance than a violent assault.[27]

Crimes against the social order accounted for only 17 percent of male crimes but nearly double that—33 percent—for women. These arrests show the porteño desire to maintain women in their proper social role in the city. Impropriety by women in a public arena could prompt arrest. For example, in October 1839, police jailed Lucía Olivera for having insulted a young girl named Eusebia Molina and for being "scandalous and quarrelsome." In June 1847, police arrested a black woman, Carmen Vásquez, for "having insulted scandalously doña Francisca Quevedo."[28] Such confrontations might also indicate class conflict between the women of the Porteño elite and working-class women who affronted them in some manner. Unless they were unduly violent, men appear to have had more latitude in committing public misdemeanors than did women. In the remaining areas of theft, gambling, and flight from the law, differences between the sexes appear minimal. Table 4 and Figure 4 provide a comparison of sexual differences in the types of crimes committed for the period from 1822 to 1850.

Women appear in the criminal-justice system proportionately more often as victims than as defendants. While more than three-fourths of violent attacks involved men against men, in about a quarter of the cases, women were victimized. Women committed crimes against men in only fourteen cases examined and against other women on nineteen occasions. Of the seventy-one crimes committed by men against women, nineteen (27 percent) were physical attacks by husbands on their wives. In her study of women and crime in colonial Buenos Aires in this volume, Susan Migden Socolow found women involved, usually as victims, in about 20 percent of criminal cases for the years 1757–97. Spanish cultural mores and laws permitted, indeed, encouraged husbands to discipline their wives with corporal punishment if they wished. Flaws

Table 4

Sexual Differences in Types of Crimes Committed, Buenos Aires, City and Province, 1822–50

Type of Crime	Percent of Total Crimes by Sex and Type			
	Males (%)	N	Females (%)	N
Attacks on Persons	38	460	21	16
Against Property	34	413	36	27
Against Social Order	17	209	33	25
Gambling	6	75	7	5
Fugitives	4	54	4	3
Totals	99*	1211	101*	76

Source: Sample 1,2.
*Rounding error.

Figure 4
Percentage of Crimes Committed by Sex and by Type,
Buenos Aires, City and Province, 1822–50

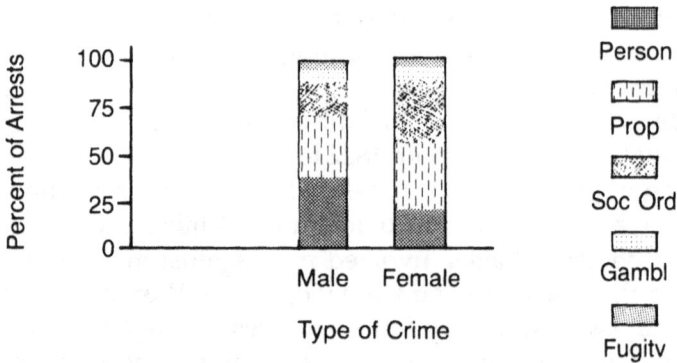

Key to Crimes

Crimes against Persons
Crimes against Property
Crimes against the Social Order
                Gambling
                Fugitives

Source: Sample 1, Sample 2.

in character or conduct could brand a wife as a woman of *mala conducta*. Society and the law countenanced the husband's exercise of virtually any measure to improve her.[29] Given the social sanction of husbands striking wives, the nineteen cases of reported wife beating doubtless represent only a tiny fraction of all such occurrences.

In one such case in early 1840, the accused made the mistake of striking his wife in the street, thereby provoking a "large scandal." This public disturbance in front of witnesses, rather than the attack per se, probably led to the arrest of the husband. In February 1844, police arrested Pablo Cuevas, a minor city official, for striking and wounding his wife with a club. He defended his action by reporting that he found his wife "drunk, causing a neighborhood scandal." Again, the public theater of the attack perhaps resulted in prosecution for an act that might have gone unpunished if committed in private.[30]

Besides wife beating, women were victims of rape. Some of the rape cases involve molestation of girls as young as four or seven. Police arrested a Portuguese man in February 1836 for raping a girl aged seven. In June 1840, the *comisario* of the fourth district of the city charged Luciano Mercante with the rape of a four-year-old girl. The social sanction of sexual aggression against adult women and the shame brought to her and her family by making the incident public militated against reporting most rape cases to authorities.[31] Child molestation would prompt arrest, whereas the rape of adult women would likely go unreported.

Viewed from a more general point of view, distinctive patterns of arrests emerge both on an annual basis and over the longer term. The proportions of the various types of crimes (property, personal attack, and so forth) remained relatively constant over time. Traced in Table 5 are the fluctuations in arrests for the period from 1827 to 1850. Arrests averaged 349 per year for the period and ranged from a low of 70 in 1844 to a high of 850 in 1830. The number of arrests shows three sharp peaks in 1830–31, 1835–36, and 1849. The largest increase coincides with Rosas's ascension to power as the governor of Buenos Aires province. He assumed the post in December 1829 and ruled the province until December 1832. His first year shows a 224 percent rise in arrests over the previous year, peaking at 850. Arrests remained high during his second year in office (760) and declined to nearer the mean in 1832 (440).[32] His return and assumption of dictatorial powers at mid-decade spurred yet another rise in arrests over the interim years when he devoted his efforts to fighting Indians on the southern frontier. Judging by the volume of arrests, Rosas richly earned his title of Restorer of the Laws. A proportion of these arrests was undoubtedly to harass his political opponents.

As he established his iron-fisted rule and brought a measure of law (albeit arbitrary) and order (albeit repressive) to the city and the province, arrests declined, reaching a low of 70 in 1844. Another rise in arrests, especially for personal assaults, occurs in 1849, but further research is necessary to interpret this third peak. It might well indicate the stirrings of political pressures and social unrest that swept the dictator from power early in 1852. Eric J. Hobsbawm

Table 5
Arrests by Year, City of Buenos Aires, 1827–50

Year	Total	vs. Persons	vs. Property	vs. Social Order	Other
1827	440	200	100	90	50
1828	440	100	110	150	80
1829	380	160	100	60	60
1830	850	330	330	110	80
1831	760	260	130	280	90
1832	440	160	170	60	50
1833	270	150	110	0	10
1834	250	110	70	60	10
1835	350	140	110	90	10
1836	420	250	80	80	10
1837	280	70	100	110	0
1838	210	80	50	70	10
1839	230	50	120	50	10
1840	150	50	50	50	0
1841-43			No Data		
1844	70	10	0	10	50
1845	110	30	20	40	20
1846	80	20	40	0	20
1847	160	40	80	40	0
1848	100	20	50	20	10
1849	320	210	40	60	10
1850	260	90	90	60	20
Mean:	310	120	91	71	29

Source: Sample 2.

concludes that natural disasters and economic and political crises give rise to increased bandit activity. Ted Gurr also finds that "sharp increases in indicators of crimes of violence and theft usually coincide with episodes of strife." The tensions and problems of the late Rosas regime might well have spurred increased crime as well as greater attempts to stop it, hence the higher number of arrests.[33]

Rosas often intervened in criminal cases, especially if they involved political security or rural order. In cases that interested him, he might read the evidence and pass judgment himself. Such a file would end with his instructions: "Shoot him," "Fine him,"

"Imprison him," "To the army." Rosas justified such direct intervention into the judicial process by citing the extraordinary powers granted him by the provincial legislature. Antonio Reyes, the Rosista aide at the Santos Lugares headquarters, also sent Rosas lists of accused prisoners, and the dictator responded with personalized punishments.[34]

Returning to the 1820s, we find sharp seasonal fluctuations in arrests. Arrests for the year 1822 show dramatic quarterly jumps for the months of April, July, and October. Table 6 and Figure 5 illustrate these peaks, which rise to about double the monthly mean of 67. In each case, the peak month increases sharply over the previous month, reaching highs of 134 in April, 128 in July, and 142, the annual high, in October. Mark D. Szuchman has concluded that such periodicity reflects the rising social disorder at a time when many workers received their quarterly wages. Rural workers often expended their quarterly earnings quickly and exuberantly at the local pulpería. Drink, gambling, and interpersonal violence reached high levels at such times.[35] Overall, the fluctuations seem to coincide with quarterly wage schedules rather than with other seasonal changes such as harvest, sheep shearing, and branding.

Table 6
Monthly Fluctuations in Number of Arrests, Buenos Aires,
City and Province, 1822

Month	Number of Arrests
January	28
February	39
March	58
April	134
May	29
June	76
July	128
August	81
September	45
October	142
November	11
December	34
Monthly Mean:	67

Source: Sample 1.

Figure 5
Monthly Fluctuations in Number of Arrests,
Buenos Aires, City and Province, 1822

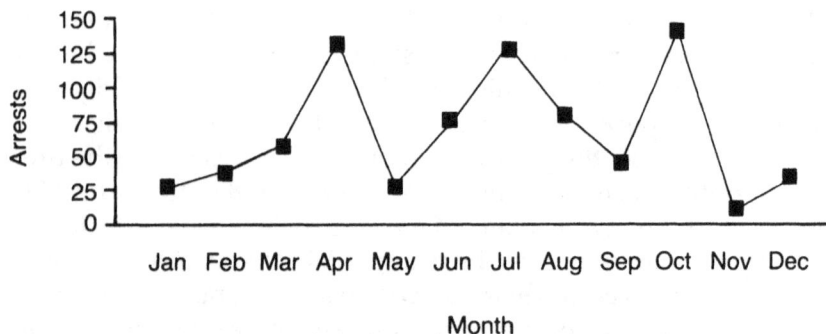

Monthly Mean = 67

Source: Sample 1.

It may also be that officials worked on a formal or informal quota system that prompted them to arrest people en masse when the quarterly quota came due. Draft quotas were routinely assigned, and officials had to fill them by "creating criminals" with a variety of innocuous, often trumped-up charges. At such times, vagrancy and passport violations provided the pretext for impressing men into military service. Official manipulation of law enforcement might have played a role in the distinctive pattern of annual arrests.[36]

Jails in Buenos Aires could only accommodate so many people. Thus, as new prisoners arrived, inmates were released to make room. Quarterly peaks in the number of prisoners set free appear in the same months of April, July, and October. In 1822, officials freed 111 persons in April (when 134 were arrested), 141 in July (128 arrests), and 121 in October (142 arrests). In contrast, only 12 prisoners were permitted to leave in March and 66 in the month of August.[37] During the high quarterly peaks, the number of people arrested and released remained approximately equal.

Punishments for crimes were not limited to incarceration and were influenced by the gender of the criminal. Of 14 women for whom the dispensation of the case is known in 1822, 12 were freed. In contrast, men were most likely to be incarcerated at the city jail or provincial presidio. About 41 percent of 437 male criminals for whom sentencing is known in 1822 received jail sentences, but 34 percent were freed. Thereafter, punishments were divided among several other options open to authorities. Nine percent of prisoners received terms of military service. Seven percent went to labor on public-works projects for a determined length of time. Three percent successfully escaped, and the remaining 6 percent suffered a variety of miscellaneous or unknown fates.[38]

Why this relative leniency in sentencing, given the fears and distrust of the porteño elite toward the unruly, threatening masses? Officials relied on the threat of arrest, not the severity or surety of punishment, to deter crime. The usual rationales for incarceration—retribution and rehabilitation—do not seem to have figured strongly in the Argentine criminal-justice system. Punishments seldom fit crimes. Instead, broader needs of the state and the elite shaped punishments. Pragmatic Unitarios and Rositas put arrested persons to work where needed and thereby increased the arbitrariness of the criminal-justice system. For the same crime, one man might receive ten years of military service and another fifteen. The need for army troops and frontier militia spurred civil and military authorities to round up rural workers and label them as vagrant to fill draft quotas. In neighboring Córdoba province during the 1830s, the government put convicted women to work building roads, making candles, and laboring for selected employers. Labor shortages, chronic at harvest and branding times on the pampa, prompted ranchers to demand stricter prosecution of vagrants. The Buenos Aires provincial Rural Code of 1865 emerged in part from decades of rancher complaints about their lack of workers.[39] Authorities tolerated and even expected certain levels of crime and violence. Given the expense of maintaining jailed prisoners and the serious labor shortages of the Río de la Plata, they did not resort to incarceration for long periods in very many cases.

As noted above, Rosas personally intervened when whim or need moved him. In 1843, for example, Manuel Donato killed a man and stole his herd of horses. After reviewing the murderer's file and noting his gaucho dress and equestrian skills, Rosas pronounced him "good for a cavalryman" and sentenced him to five years of military service. More detailed, longitudinal analysis will determine the degree to which arrests varied with labor and military needs.[40]

Based on the analysis of crime in four major cities, Ted Gurr also found that "labor scarcity is an incentive to exploit criminals' labor, even to create 'criminals' to undertake unpleasant tasks." He concludes that "insofar as political elites are directly threatened by social disorder, they are almost certain to attempt to control it by whatever means come to hand." They will meet perceived threats to their property, personal safety, and social position "by any legal or institutional means available." The arrest and incarceration records for Buenos Aires seem to confirm this conclusion. Both Unitario and Rosista elites used the selective application of the law to protect their interests from perceived dangers of the rural and urban working class. Aside from minimizing the real losses and injuries suffered through theft and assault, officials in Buenos Aires also reinforced the existing social hierarchy in both city and countryside.[41]

Appendix

Sample 1, consisting of 810 cases, is technically a universe of all prisoners held during the year 1822 at the provincial presidio (24 percent of the total), the military prison (24 percent), and the city jail (52 percent). Most of the prisoners had been arrested in 1822 (722), but 69 remained from the previous year, 9 from 1820, 3 from 1819, and one each from 1818, 1816, and 1814, with 4 cases unknown. The data come from quarterly reports recorded on large, two-by-three foot summary sheets housed under: Estadística: Repartición y establecimientos públicos, 1822, AGN X 12–7–6. Useful data from the records include sex, race, legal status, age, occupation, and civil (marital) status of the prisoner; nature of the crime; and disposition of the case. Officials recorded birthplace for only 153 of the 810 cases. This would seem to indicate that officials did not consider birthplace a very significant statistic compared with race or occupation for which data are much more complete.

Valid Cases, 1822 Prisoner Data

Variable	Valid Cases	Unknown or Missing
Place of Incarceration	810	0
Age	810	0
Sex	810	0
Race	776	34
Civil (Marital) Status	765	45
Occupation	745	75
Type of Crime	734	76
Legal Status (free or slave)	691	119
Birthplace	153	657

Sample 2 consists of 657 cases from a summary index of police reports compiled by Rafael Trelles. Every tenth arrest (as opposed to total entries, which include other incidents not resulting in arrest) was coded from the index for the years 1827 to 1850. No report was found for the year 1841. The years 1842 and 1843 were omitted because reports failed to distinguish between urban and rural crimes. The reports are housed under Rafael Trelles, "Indice del Archivo del Departamento General de Policía, desde el año de 1812," vol. 1, 1812–30, AGN X 44–9–39, vol. 2, 1831–50, AGN X 44–9–40 (vol. 3, 1853–70, AGN X 27–31–1 was not sampled). Useful variables include month and year of arrest, sex, race, legal status of the criminal, nature of the crime; and sex, race, and relationship of the victim to the accused. Total arrests for the years can be computed by multiplying the 10 percent sample by 10.

Valid Cases, Arrest Data, 1827–50

Variable	Valid Cases	Unknown or Missing
Month of Arrest	657	0
Year of Arrest	657	0
Sex	657	0
Type of Crime	657	0
Sex of Victim	361	296
Relationship of Victim to Accused	76	581
Race of Accused	67	590
Race of Victim	37	620
Legal Status of Accused	33	624

Notes

The authors thank the following institutions for research support for this study: The Fulbright-Hays Doctoral Research Program, the Social Science Research Council, and the Faculty Research and Professional Development Program of North Carolina State University at Raleigh.

1. Clifton B. Kroeber, "Rosas and the Revision of Argentine History, 1880–1955," *Inter-American Review of Bibliography* (Jan. 1960), 4–5, 14, 17, 21–22; Leonardo Paso et al., *Corrientes historiográficas* (Buenos Aires, 1974), pp. 41–46.

2. Ted Robert Gurr, *Rogues, Rebels, and Reformers* (Beverly Hills, 1976), pp. 180–81; see also Ted Robert Gurr, Peter N. Grabosky, and Richard C. Hula, *The Politics of Crime and Conflict: A Comparative History of Four Cities* (Beverly Hills, 1977). On Unitario-Rosista continuities, see Richard W. Slatta, "Rural Criminality and Social Conflict in Nineteenth-Century Buenos Aires Province," *Hispanic American Historical Review* (Aug. 1980), 452, 455, 469, 471; Mark D. Szuchman, "Continuity and Conflict in Buenos Aires: Comments on the Historical City," in Stanley R. Ross and Thomas F. McGann, eds., *Buenos Aires: 400 Years* (Austin, 1982), pp. 53–54, 59–60; and Szuchman, "Disorder and Social Control in Buenos Aires, 1810–1860," *Journal of Interdisciplinary History* (Summer 1984), 83–110.

3. Emeric Essex Vidal, *Picturesque Illustrations of Buenos Ayres and Montevideo* (London, 1820), pp. 8–9; John Lynch, *Argentine Dictator: Juan Manuel de Rosas, 1829–1852* (Oxford, 1981), p. 127; population figures from Benito Díaz, *Rosas, Buenos Aires y la organización nacional* (Buenos Aires, 1974), pp. 154, 264.

4. Vidal, *Picturesque Illustrations*, pp. 15–16; quotation from pp. 61–62; Richard W. Slatta, "Pulperías and Contraband Capitalism in Nineteenth-Century Buenos Aires Province," *The Americas* (Jan. 1982) 347–62. On contraband trade, see Sergio Villalobos R., *Comercio y contrabando en el Río de la Plata y Chile, 1700–1811* (Buenos Aires, 1965), pp. 45–47, 97–100, 107–13; Jonathan C. Brown, *A Socioeconomic History of Argentina, 1776–1860* (Cambridge, 1979), pp. 9–10, 21–26; and Brown, "Outpost to Entrepôt: Trade and Commerce at Colonial Buenos Aires," in Ross and McGann, *Buenos Aires*, pp. 5–11.

5. Jorge A. Bossio, *Historia de las pulperías* (Buenos Aires, 1972), pp. 135, 253; Slatta, "Pulperías," pp. 349–54; Vidal, *Picturesque illustrations*, p. 23; José Antonio Wilde, *Buenos Aires desde setenta años atras (1810–1880)* (Buenos Aires, 1966), pp. 158, 237–39; quotation from Alexander Caldcleugh, *Travels in South America during the years 1819–20–21*, 2 vols. (London, 1825), I: 179–80.

6. Police report of 17 Jan. 1827 in Rafael Trelles, "Indice del Archivo

del Departamento General de Policía, desde el año de 1812," 3 vols. (Buenos Aires, n.d.), I: bk. 22, fol. 44, AGN X 44–9–39. The Trelles "Indice" is a manuscript document compiled over a long period of time.

7. La Razón, *Historia viva*, p. 12; Francisco L. Romay, *Historia de la Policía Federal Argentina*, 6 vols. (Buenos Aires, 1963–75), II: 34–39, 83; Tulio Halperín Donghi, *Politics, Economics and Society in Argentina in the Revolutionary Period*, trans. Richard Southern (Cambridge, 1975), pp. 50–51; Szuchman, "Continuity and Conflict," p. 59. On the police elsewhere, see Eric H. Monkkonen, *Police in Urban America, 1860–1920* (Cambridge, 1981), p. 151; and Gurr, *Rogues*, p. 124.

8. La Razón, *Historia viva*, p. 16; document of 11 June 1822 in Trelles, "Indice," I: bk. 4, doc. 245, AGN X 44–9–39.

9. Francisco L. Romay, *Los serenos de Buenos Aires (policía nocturna), años 1834–1872* (Buenos Aires, 1947), pp. 17–18, 21–22, 27–28, 49–50; Wilde, *Buenos Aires*, pp. 150, 157; La Razón, *Historia viva*, p. 25; Romay, *Historia*, II: 143–44.

10. Police report of 22 Oct. 1847 in Trelles, "Indice." II: bk. 178, fol. 15, AGN X 44–9–40; samples 1 and 2 (see Appendix for descriptions and limitations of samples of criminal records).

Sample 1 and 2. The percentages of males by marital status totals 101 percent because of rounding error. Peter C. Hoffer, "Counting Crime in Premodern England and America: A Review Essay," *Historical Methods* (Fall 1981), 187; V. A. C. Gatrell and T. B. Hadden, "Criminal Statistics and Their Interpretation," in Edward A. Wrigley, ed., *Nineteenth-Century Society: Essays in the Use of Quantitative Methods for the Study of Social Data* (Cambridge, 1972), p. 350; Gurr, *Politics of Crime and Conflict*, pp. 17–19. On the condition of the rural family, see Richard W. Slatta, *Gauchos and the Vanishing Frontier* (Lincoln, 1983), ch. 4.

It is recognized that the official statistics examined reflect jailings for 1822 and arrests for the period 1827–50, rather than the actual incidence of criminal acts committed (the so-called "dark figure"). While not providing an exact measure of actual crime, the official figures help to gauge variations (and consistencies) in official attitudes toward crime. In general, the official numbers better reflect the true incidence of serious crimes and are less reliable for petty crimes. With this caveat, we refer to criminality and the commission of crimes as reflected (understated to be sure) in the official figures.

11. Sample 1; Sample 2; Ricardo Rodríguez Molas, *Historia social del gaucho* (Buenos Aires, 1968), p. 171.

12. Evelyn P. Stevens, "*Marianismo*: The Other Face of *Machismo* in Latin America," in Ann Pescatello, ed., *Female and Male in Latin America: Essays* (Pittsburgh, 1973), p. 95.

13. Halperín Donghi, *Politics*, pp. 50, 57; Rodríguez Molas, *Historia social*, pp. 46, 161–72; Slatta, "Rural Criminality," pp. 461–63.

14. Sample 1; Slatta, *Gauchos*, p. 64.

15. Sample 1; Slatta, *Gauchos*, pp. 106, 110–18, 193.

16. Slatta, "Rural Criminality," p. 453; Madaline Wallace Nichols, *The Gaucho: Cattle Hunter, Cavalryman, Ideal of Romance* (New York, 1968), pp. 4, 17. See the discussion of frontier violence by Silvio R. Duncan Baretta and John Markoff, "Civilization and Barbarism: Cattle Frontiers in Latin America," *Comparative Studies in Society and History* (Oct. 1978), 592–93, 606–607. On the "dangerous classes," see Monkkonen, *Police*, pp. 20–23, 87–88; and Louis Chevalier, *Laboring Classes and Dangerous Classes In Paris During the First Half of the Nineteenth Century*, trans. Frank Jellinek (New York, 1973).

17. Sample 1.

18. George Reid Andrews, *The Afro-Argentines of Buenos Aires, 1800–1900* (Madison, 1980), pp. 54–58, 146; Lynch, *Argentine Dictator*, pp. 119–20; sample 1; police report of 7 June 1831 in Trelles, "Indice," II: bk. 50, fol. 66, AGN X 44–9–40.

19. Decree of 19 Dec. 1826 in Trelles, "Indice," I: bk. 16, fol. 231, AGN X 44–9–39; order dated 27 May 1826 in Trelles, "Indice," I: bk. 18, fol. 65, AGN X 44–9–39.

20. Andrews, *Afro-Argentines*, pp. 8–9, 66, 83–84.

21. Andrews, *Afro-Argentines*, pp. 97–99, 146–47, 157–60; decree of 1 Feb. 1822 in Trelles, "Indice," I: bk. 4, fol. 45; decree of 19 Feb. 1823 in Trelles, "Indice," I: bk. 6, fol. 97; order of 21 June 1825 in Trelles, "Indice," I: bk. 12, fol. 164; AGN X 44–9–39; Lynch, *Argentine Dictator*, pp. 121–24.

22. Nancy Caro Hollander, "Women in the Political Economy of Argentina" (PhD diss., UCLA, 1974), pp. 17, 24–25, 29, 31; see also Hollander, "Women: The Forgotten Half of Argentine History," in Pescatello, ed., *Female and Male*, pp. 141–58.

23. Sample 1 and 2; (for females as victims, sample 2); Dretha M. Phillips and Lois B. DeFleur, "Gender Ascription and the Stereotyping of Deviants," *Criminology* (Nov. 1982), 431–48.

24. Sample 1 and 2.

25. Sample 1; Halperín Donghi, *Politics*, p. 381.

26. Sample 1; Slatta, "Rural Criminality," pp. 465–67; Slatta, "Pulperías," pp. 358–61; Romay, *Historia*, II: 31–33. On the difficult problem of determining real, or "dark," crime as opposed to officially recorded crime, see Gurr, *Rogues*, pp. 20–21; and Gatrell and Hadden, "Criminal Statistics," pp. 355, 361.

27. Sample 1 and 2.

28. Sample 1 and 2; report of 31 Oct. 1839 in Trelles, "Indice," II: bk.

116, fol. 125; report of 10 June 1847 in Trelles, "Indice," II: bk. 149, fol. 51, AGN X 44–9–40.

29. Sample 2; Susan M. Socolow, "Women and Crime: Buenos Aires, 1757–97," *Journal of Latin American Studies* (May 1980), 41, 43, 45.

30. Report of 31 Jan. 1840 in Trelles, "Indice," II: bk. 123, fol. 23; report of 26 Feb. 1844 in Trelles, "Indice," II; bk. 132, fol. 67, AGN X 44–9–40.

31. Report of 28 Feb. 1836 in Trelles, "Indice," II: bk. 90, fol. 61; report of 15 June 1840 in Trelles, "Indice," II: bk. 123, fol. 115, AGN X 44–9–40; Socolow, "Women and Crime," pp. 46–47.

32. Sample 2.

33. Eric J. Hobsbawm, *Bandits* (New York, 1981), p. 22. Given the imprecision of population figures for Buenos Aires, no attempt is made to estimate annual arrest rates.

34. Quotation from Lynch, *Politics*, p. 169; see also pp. 211–12; Romay *Los serenos*, p. 118.

35. Sample 1; Szuchman, "Disorder and Social Control," passim. For examples of the quarterly payment schedule of rural peons, see wage records for the estancias of Juan Manuel de Rosas, July-Sept. 1843, AGN X 26–4–2; and Apr.-June 1849, AGN X 26–8–4.

36. Slatta, *Gauchos*, pp. 112, 129–30.

37. Sample 1.

38. Sample 1.

39. Slatta, "Rural Criminality," pp. 456–60; Donna J. Guy, "Women, Peonage, and Industrialization: Argentina, 1810–1914," *Latin American Research Review* (1981), 60.

40. Slatta, *Gauchos*, pp. 111–12, 117, 128–29.

41. Gurr, *Rogues*, pp. 149, 176. Compare the findings of Julia Kirk Blackwelder and Lyman L. Johnson, "Changing Criminal Patterns in Buenos Aires, 1890–1914," *Journal of Latin American Studies* (Nov. 1982), 359–80.

3

Violence For Show

Knife Dueling on a Nineteenth-Century Cattle Frontier

John Charles Chasteen

Many English and American readers first encountered gauchos in the fiction of William H. Hudson (1841–1922). Though he wrote in English, Hudson was born and raised in the Province of Buenos Aires, where his father kept a pulpería, or country store and tavern. As a young man, he roamed the pampa alone, collecting wildlife specimens for the Smithsonian Institution. He knew the rural people well and wrote about them with sensitivity in his first book, *The Purple Land that England Lost: Travels and Adventures in the Banda Oriental, South America* (1885). Based on Hudson's experiences across the Río de la Plata in Uruguay, the story purports to show English-speaking readers what life was like in that part of South America before the coming of "the iron-shod monster named Progress."[1]

Richard, the young protagonist of the book, goes searching for work on an estancia and learns to get along among the gauchos. In order to test his strength, one of them soon provokes a knife fight with him, using the *facón*, the foot-long blade each gaucho carried thrust diagonally under his belt at the small of his back. The fight ends suddenly when Richard manages to graze his attacker's cheek, and later, new friends congratulate him. His enemy will never bother him again, and the authorities will not question him about the incident, because he is a foreigner and cannot be forced to serve in the army. Soon, though, it will be necessary for him to kill someone, since several fighters are already planning to challenge him. "In your next fight," he is told, "you must not wound, but kill, or you will have no peace."[2]

Is this realistic? Would men risk their lives to pick fights with total strangers, and if so, why? An attempt to answer these questions will be made by looking closely at a number of actual knife duels preserved in detailed eyewitness accounts from the criminal archives of the borderland between Uruguay and Rio Grande do Sul, the southernmost Brazilian state in some ways so much like Uruguay and Argentina.[3] Most of the evidence comes from the tumultuous middle years of the nineteenth century, when civil wars swept across the borderland in seemingly endless waves. It will be seen first of all that violence was not an exception for the people who lived there, but part of their everyday lives, and next, that they used violence as an expression as well as a tool. It will be necessary to distinguish clearly between these symbolic uses of violence and its more familiar instrumental uses, approaching the criminal archives of the nineteenth-century borderland with the attitude of an anthropologist and paying most attention to how violence was interpreted by the borderlanders themselves.[4] It will become evident that Hudson's description is quite realistic.

The Violent Tenor of Life on a Cattle Frontier

The scene was a rural pulpería (in Portuguese, *venda*) on the plains of Brazil's southern frontier in 1829. Inside the construction of wooden-frame and sun-dried mud daub, men from the surrounding estancias gathered to talk and drink. Behind the counter the *pulpero*, or storekeeper, dispensed cane liquor, black tobacco twisted like lengths of rope, sugar, Paraguayan tea leaves, hats, ponchos, and piece goods by the yard. On the rough boards of the counter, carved with initials, dates, and cattle brands, stood the scales with its weights and a bundle of brown wrapping paper, and to one side, the account book in which the pulpero kept tabs. Almost all the business was done on credit, and the pulpero seldom had much money in cash.[5] A young Indian and his employer sat drinking together when the conversation turned to a horse the Indian was breaking. The employer, who owned the horse, objected to the Indian's rough approach to breaking the animal. Growing quite angry, he shouted that it was the boy, not the horse, who deserved beating, and he proceeded to batter the boy with the flat of his sword. It was a fatal mistake. The boy pulled his facón and drove it into his attacker's heart, killing him instantly.[6]

A second scene occurred in July 1831. The sky had hung heavy as gray slate for weeks; it had rained incessantly; and an icy wind blew across the sere, rolling plains. The República Oriental del Uruguay had just come into existence the year before, following an end to the long struggle against the Brazilian invaders, and contingents of the defeated militia of Rio Grande do Sul were still loosely massed in the borderland. Manuel Luís Osório, future hero of the Paraguayan War, received news of a killing among militiamen in his jurisdiction of the Chapel of Santana do Livramento. It happened at a pulpería twenty-five miles north of the border on the banks of the Iguatiá. Osório went to the spot and took the testimony of thirty men concerning the case. This is what he learned.[7]

Among the men gathered at the venda on the day of the killing had been two who were known enemies: Antônio Dias and Gaspar Alves Bueno. Several of the witnesses said that the two had "antecedents," past differences, but none thought it pertinent to say what those differences were, if they knew at all, and Osório did not ask. Virtually any borderlander had enemies. A man was partly measured by the importance of his enemies, so they were to some extent cultivated.[8] Bueno talked often and loudly about the two men he had already killed. Over a period of years, several witnesses had heard Bueno say he was going to kill Dias "because [Dias] thought he was so tough," and one had seen him carve two crosses on a cart to seal his promise to kill Dias. On the day of the killing, however, Dias and Bueno had arrived together at the venda and begun to drink wine. One witness thought he had seen Bueno secretly loosening his facón. Then, without warning or argument, Bueno drew his blade and opened Dias's belly with a fatal slash. Dias rose and reached for his own facón, but, too weak, he turned and stumbled ten paces out the door of the venda, holding in his entrails, and collapsed on the ground. One witness, who was just riding up at that moment, asked Bueno what had happened. Bueno replied that it was he, Gaspar Bueno, who had killed Dias and that "there was nothing wrong with it." Another man who was there told Bueno to leave, and Bueno mounted but then dismounted to ensure he had killed Dias. Dias cried: "Senhor Gaspar, why do you want to kill me? What have I done to you? Aren't you satisfied yet?" Bueno spat: "The devil! You're still talking?" and sat down on Dias's chest, slashing the dying man's face eighteen times while the other men watched.[9]

Although the sheer intensity of this violence is shocking, the shock must be ignored in order to see what such scenes meant for the spectators. The Brazilian-Uruguayan borderland was a cattle frontier, and the principal element of the diet was meat, often unaccompanied even by salt. Because of the material circumstances of their lives, borderlanders had the habit of slaughter. Any man who lived on an estancia was quite naturally accustomed to cutting the throats of sheep and cattle for his own table, and this was done with very much the same emotion with which any other unpleasant but routine and necessary task was done. In 1887, an English traveler in northern Uruguay watched two small boys cut the throat of a dog. When he protested the brutality of the act, they hastened to reassure him that it was their dog.[10]

Human throats were cut in precisely the same fashion, especially during the civil wars. The *guerra gaucha*, as it was called, relied on speed and surprise. It was a light-cavalry guerrilla war with no place for prisoners. Firearms were so scarce that most rebels never fired a shot, but did their fighting with lances and *boleadoras* (three tethered stones that whirl through the air to tangle in an animal's legs). In order to save ammunition, they executed prisoners with a single dexterous but massive cut from ear to ear, the *degüello* (in Portuguese, *degola*). The degüello was much feared, mostly because it was considered shameful to be slaughtered like a cow. Practically it was at least a quick death and might even be applied to end the suffering of a comrade in arms during this period of incessant warfare.

These years saw three colonial wars between the Spanish and Portuguese empires (1763–1801); the Uruguayan Wars of Independence, including multiple Brazilian interventions (1810–28); ten-year civil wars in both Uruguay and Rio Grande do Sul (1835–52), ending with another Brazilian intervention (repeated yet again in 1863–65); the major Paraguayan War (1865–70), in which both Uruguay and Brazil participated; the Uruguayan Revolution of the Lances (1870–72); the Brazilian Federalist Revolution (1893–95); the Uruguayan Revolutions of 1897 and 1904; and the Brazilian Revolution of 1923.

Of the four men involved in the two killings described earlier, only the Indian boy was not a part-time soldier. Even so, as were all borderlanders, he was an expert at killing with a knife. He had a clear motive: the other man was beating him and he struck in anger. It was probably not the first time he had been beaten by the man at whose house he lived, but the two seemed to get along well enough before the argument. Since they were drinking together, could it have been the liquor? Men always drank at pulperías, and doubtless the drink made them pugnacious. In 1863, two drunks in an Uruguayan pulpería kept attempting to fight one another until the pulpero took their knives away. One was so besotted that he tumbled from his horse on the way home and died of a concussion. Inebriation, however, falls far short of a complete explanation of the fighting. In 1860, another pulpero commented that the attacker had drunk "just enough to have an excuse."[11] Drunkenness was an extenuating circumstance before the law, and it was often feigned, both for that reason and to fool the adversary, but fighting drunk was a good way to get killed. A few precautions were in order when one entered a pulpería.

In 1867, more than half the criminal cases in one Uruguayan borderland county were cases of murder. In 1878, the police chief of the borderland county of Cerro Largo, with a population of about 25,000, reported 31 violent deaths in the previous two years. Figures for Uruguay as a whole are not available until 1886. In that year there were 763 arrests for theft and robbery and 1,591 for physical assault, including 127 murders. Authorities of the Brazilian province of Rio Grande do Sul handled 1,987 criminal cases in the 1860s; somewhat more than one-tenth involved crimes against property, while fully two-thirds involved physical assault for other reasons.[12] Violence was a common coin of social relationships in borderland society, and the police were as often as not notorious ruffians themselves.

Violence for Show

Probably what most compelled the Indian boy to stab the his employer was the humiliation of being beaten in a public place, for pulperías were, above all, public places. The inhabitants of isolated estancias seldom saw each other except there. A crowded pulpería was full of spectators, and public recognition of valor was extremely important to these men. The man the Indian boy killed seems to have had only a small herd and no land. Still, the social distance between him and his hired hand was significant. The boy's refusal to be whipped like a dog in front of others was a bid for a rough equality with them, but the fact that he was an

Indian made this a desperate bid. His blow was not merely a slash on the cheek calculated to establish dominance. That would have been suicide, given the race stratification of the society in which he lived.

The killing of Dias was extremely theatrical. Bueno arrived at the pulpería with Dias, planning to kill him in front of witnesses. Bueno was a big talker and needed some substantiation. The slashing of Dias's face was strictly for show, a ritual destruction of the fallen man's social identity, completing the crushing victory Bueno took pains to publicize. As for other motives, Dias himself seemed to know of none, and neither did any of the thirty witnesses called to testify. Many of these had known the two men for years.

The need to defend himself against public insult is clear in the case of an Italian pulpero, Giovanni Arvigo. This shopkeeper in the town of Melo marched one day into the office of the military commander of Cerro Largo to say that "he had just been insulted in his house (pulpería) by the traveler Gregorio Naranjo in such terms that he was obliged to take out his pistol and shoot him." It was 1838, year of the French Intervention against Juan Manuel de Rosas. Arvigo and a French doctor had been at lunch when an Argentine stranger appeared who identified himself as an officer, though he had apparently not served in some time. The Italian and the Frenchman invited the Argentine for a drink, which he declined. The Europeans took offense. The conversation escalated from comments about "stiff-necked Argentines with nothing in their pockets" and observations on the unflattering traits shared by Englishmen, Frenchmen, and Italians to the point where Arvigo had pulled out his pistol and fired.[13]

A similar quarrel between strangers occurred in 1869 at the pulpería of a young Basque, Fermín Galarraga, situated by the important ford in the Río Tacuarí, El Paso del Dragón. Two brothers, José and Felipe Flores, were out back playing *tejo*, a game rather like horseshoes. They were in their late twenties, living on the property of their brother-in-law about twenty-five miles west, and had probably just taken some cattle to market in Brazil. They had two gold pesos bet on a close toss when Viríssimo Acosta, a man neither they nor the pulpero knew, rode up. The Flores brothers asked Acosta to pass judgment on the toss in question. Taking up a straw,

Acosta measured the positions of the two tiles and pronounced them equally close to the stake. This meant that the two pesos stayed in the pot for the next toss, and the Flores brothers asked Acosta to remain as judge. Acosta replied haughtily that they were not speaking to a man such as themselves and should learn how to address him. Felipe Flores asked to know his name, and Acosta pronounced it, whereupon Felipe replied that he found nothing in that name but a man like the rest. Acosta drew the saber that hung at his thigh, Felipe took out his facón, and the two circled while the pulpero tried to separate them.

Meanwhile, José Flores, furious at Acosta's airs, rushed into the pulpería, grabbed his facón, and charged Acosta with such energy that he stumbled backward over some stacked tiles and fell. José leapt on him and pinned him down, but the worried pulpero persuaded him to let the saber-carrying stranger free, because he might be a vecino, an important man of the neighborhood. At this, José seems to have shown his disdain for Acosta by turning his back, because Acosta leapt up and killed him with a single saber stroke. Felipe then attacked his brother's killer and managed to wound him once. Not surprisingly, given the inequality of their arms, he received four wounds in return, including a slash on the face and the loss of three fingers. Acosta mounted and rode away. Felipe tried to follow, but was too weak to ride and had to return to the pulpería.[14]

Occurring between strangers, cases such as these clearly bring out the symbolic aspects of borderland violence. The documents repeatedly tell curiously straightforward stories of men who fought for what seem to be trivial reasons. Sometimes the men were enemies, like Dias and Bueno, but often one had simply insulted the other's name, given him a shove, or dared him to back up his brag. Such is the information the witnesses, investigators, and judges thought explanatory. The man who had issued the challenge was considered legally at fault. The witnesses established that and then went on to tell about the fight they had watched, often without interfering. There was apparently at issue a matter that all of them understood implicity, but what was it?

A Matter of Honor

The prickliness of the Italian pulpero Arvigo or of the saber-carrying Acosta was a matter of honor. Poorly understood today, the system of honor formed a vital part of the social psychology of the nineteenth-century borderland. Quite the opposite of an "honor system," which proposes that the inner conscience govern behavior, the historical system of honor depended above all on external referents in determining behavior. This is why in traditional Hispanic societies, unmarried women were not expected to govern their own impulses, but were always chaperoned; their honor had to be guaranteed and the care taken with it demonstrated. Demonstration was vital, because the state of one's honor did not depend on an inner voice, but on public reputation. It was the iron law of *"el qué dirán,"* literally "what others will say." Honor was the link between collective standards and individual performance. It was a measure of how well a person was playing his role in life, and each actor judged the excellence of his performance by the response of the audience.[15]

Arvigo told the military commander that he had been obliged to shoot the stranger who had walked into his pulpería and insulted him in front of his friends. He fully expected that the military commander would find his action justified. Otherwise, everyone would have said that Arvigo had allowed himself to be insulted, a breach of the accepted standards of male behavior. Far more than a momentary humiliation, the result would have been a public disgrace, and Arvigo's worth as a man reduced in the eyes of his neighbors and customers. Arvigo did not have to tell the commander all this; it was common knowledge. The same was true in the case of the two Flores brothers and Viríssimo Acosta. When Felipe Flores told Acosta that "he found nothing in that name but a man like the rest," he was issuing a direct challenge to Acosta's honor. By his saber and his airs, it can be inferred that Acosta's family was upper class. The position he was brought up to fulfill was one that demanded deference from men such as the Flores brothers. He was angered by their familiarity with him and told them that they were not speaking to a man such as themselves and should learn how to address him.

Though the structure of the system of honor was generally the same, the role an individual actor was expected to play varied according to the social script, and scripts varied widely in time and place, according to the position of the individual in the social matrix. The honor of men was always quite different from the honor of women, for example, because their roles were different. The chastity important as a standard for women's honor would have been vaguely dishonorable in a man, who was expected to demonstrate virility. The honor of men in the nineteenth-century borderland depended on how well they upheld the standards of the groups in which they sought recognition. While the Indian boy José demanded recognition only as a man who must not be whipped like a dog in a public place, Viríssimo Acosta demanded recognition as a superior. Gaspar Bueno demanded recognition as a dangerous killer; Arvigo as an upstanding shopkeeper and a patriotic member of the Uruguay's Italian colony.

Culture Group and Social Class

The primary function of symbolic violence was to arbitrate a man's place in a particular social group, but for each man, the group varied. The same violence might have different meaning for different groups. Knife fighting probably would have been thuggery in the eyes of Giovanni Arvigo and European associates like the French physician with whom he was having lunch. These were townsmen, and they dressed, talked, and lived quite differently from rural borderlanders. Their standards of honor were accordingly different. Incidents between pulperos and customers were not common. The pulpero's place in the pulpería was well defined, and he did not compete with the men on the other side of the counter. The Italian shopkeeper, like most pulperos, kept a pistol handy.

Arvigo shot not a rude gaucho but an educated officer, a foreigner like himself, who had entered Arvigo's store to buy sweets for a sick friend. Foreigners tended to fight each other, most often with civil suits rather than knives or pistols. The charge was generally slander, and the purpose was vindication of honor. The standards of town-dwelling shopkeepers and artisans emphasized qualities other than physical dominance. A different definition of honor was clearly at work when a shopkeeper accused his clerk of stealing and the clerk sued to defend his commercial reputation, in his words, "his only capital."[16]

Lawyers, pharmacists, doctors, agronomists, notaries, and other townsmen also dueled with verbose thrusts and parries in the public forum provided by local newspapers. Being sensitive matters of honor, these prolix encounters could be unbelievably protracted. They might begin with ceremonious hat doffing to "the scintillating pen of the noble adversary," or with dark allusions to infamy in high places, never mentioning names. Uruguayan customs inspector Osvaldo Cervetti would not stoop to knife fighting, but in the newspapers he could be quite feisty. He occasionally worked himself up to such a white heat in defense of his honor that he wrote blistering responses to the letters of his own supporters.[17] Most rural borderlanders had no interest at all in this sort of competition. The men who gathered in front of the counter of a pulpería considered legal recourse dishonorable in itself, an admission of physical impotence. In their view, delaying revenge and making the insult an official affair would only have publicized and prolonged the humiliation. Their standards required that a man react to insults with violence to maintain his standing in the group.[18]

Thus, the cultural boundary between rural borderlanders and townsmen (including some rural pulperos) was important in determining the two styles of conflict. Since early in the nineteenth century, borderlanders had made a conscious distinction between men like themselves and everyone else. By the close of the century, the word gaucho had come to designate a culture group defined principally by horsemanship. Anyone who handled a horse (and by extension a facón and boleadora) like a gaucho was classed as such. Everyone else formed the other group. In Portuguese, men who were not gaúchos were called *bahianos*, in reference to the northern province from which they were assumed indiscriminately to have come. In Spanish, they were *maturrangos*, as a French traveler in Uruguay heard himself disparagingly called in 1820.[19] Such a distinction is common in equestrian cultures, of course, having emerged in the epithet "dude" even during the brief period of true cowboy culture in the Great Plains of North America. A gaucho had scant interest in fighting a townsman, whose defeat would demonstrate nothing. In order for the competition to make sense, both players had to be in the same league.[20]

The distinction between gauchos and maturrangos or bahianos cut across lines of class and race stratification without erasing them. Even owners of huge borderland estancias often lived in a manner very much like other rural borderlanders who had no land. In 1880, one of the richest men in the county of Cerro Largo, Francisco Saraiva do Amaral, the owner of six estancias and many thousands of cattle, lived in a house with three small rooms and a packed earth floor. His furnishings were a long pine table with twelve chairs, four larger chairs with arms, one iron bedstead, eight mattresses, and two trunks.[21] Townspeople of fairly modest means had a higher standard of comfort than this.

The Saraiva do Amaral children had little schooling. The boys wore the gaucho *chiripá*, a garment of Indian origin, around the estancia, and they worked beside the hired hands. They practiced knife fighting among themselves and with their cousins. According to family recollections, the eldest once crossed blades with a landless black man who was a well-known fighter and was saved by his father when the fight went against him.[22]

This encounter illustrates the tensions in the overlap of class and culture group. The estanciero's son considered the black gaucho a worthy foe, and so he was, but had the fight developed differently, the landless black man would have had no powerful father to intervene. Acosta, the haughty stranger from Brazil, was saved from the Flores brothers by the solicitous pulpero. Obviously, such an intervention on the behalf of a rich estanciero might make him into a valuable friend. The hierarchy of class and race distinctions was inexorable, and it was clearly a key reference point in questions of honor, but in the moment when the knives were out, a savage equality reigned. Acosta was obligated to fight to maintain his honor at the pulpería, and he might not always be as lucky as he was that day. The attacker of the Indian boy José would never again saberwhip a hired hand. Even borderland slaves often went mounted and armed and reacted to a challenge in much the same manner as their masters. In 1839, a dispute over horses claimed by two different masters (neither of whom was present) led the slave Gabriel to attack two other slaves. Brandishing his pistol in one hand and his long blade in the other, he said, "Now either you kill me or I am going to kill one of you!"[23]

Cultural identity and the generalized capacity for violence put limits on class exploitation. A landowner's *agregado* families, who lived and kept animals on his property, provided him personal followers in time of war. Even in time of peace, an estancia required defense and constant vigilance. The most important task on an estancia was guarding its wealth on the hoof, so that in principle, excessive exploitation of labor made little sense.

The most valuable part of the animals was the hide, and consequently animals slaughtered to feed the agregados of the estancia still brought a good profit for the landowner. Profits were limited, however, by the inelastic market for hides and jerked beef, and consequently capital accumulation was slow. The subdivision of landowning through inheritance produced estancias of all sizes, and even agregados without land often had their own herds. In the property-tax list of 1860, 137 estancieros in Cerro Largo held assets valued at 1,390,469 pesos, while their 189 agregados with herds held assets valued at 338,531 pesos, a quarter as much. The richest of the agregados declared 13,302 pesos, more than the mean wealth of the landowners (10,149 pesos).[24] For all these reasons, the levels of the social hierarchy were blurred, and the common cultural identity of rural borderlanders was strengthened.

Honor or Interest?

Even in the fairly rare case records in which two borderlanders seem to be fighting over material goods, the prize seems more important as a symbol than anything else. This was clearly the case in a fight that occurred in a Cerro Largo pulpería in 1869 between a twenty-eight-year-old local named Pío Videla and Florentino Gómez, a drifter from Argentina. Gómez was an agregado on a nearby estancia, but Videla worked as a day laborer and lived in one of the back rooms of the pulpería. For some time, the men had quarreled over a mare and a cow belonging to Gómez. Videla had sold the animals with the permission of Gómez, so he claimed; Gómez denied it vehemently. Now the animals were gone, and

Gómez fumed about it as daily he entered the pulpería where Videla roomed. The young Spaniard behind the counter and other men at the pulpería had heard Gómez declare repeatedly over a period of weeks that Videla was a rogue and would pay with his life. One day Gómez arrived, asked for a glass of cane liquor, downed it, and walked boldly into Videla's room. He found Videla chopping tobacco for a cigarette with a double-edged, silver-handled blade twenty inches long. The fight was bloody, and both men were wounded before they were separated.[25]

Gómez died of his wounds within a day or two. He paid a high price for a cow worth about six pesos and a mare worth about two (borderlanders refused to ride mares). This is especially so, since the minimum wealth declared by a agregado with animals in the property tax of 1860 was 71 pesos, and the mean was 1,791 pesos. Gómez did not attack Videla because of the material value of the two animals, but because of what they symbolized. Their sale meant that Videla had misused him without penalty and the disgrace was public. It is not recorded that Gómez ever once asked to be paid for the animals. He knew he had to fight to show that he was able to defend his interests and avenge insults, or his reputation—doubly in question since he was not a local—would be shattered. Then, other men would begin to test the limits of his powerlessness. There would be more insults, and he would lose more animals. Videla was a tough character, and Gómez was obviously afraid of him. Far from being irrational, as it might have seemed at first, the death of Florentino Gómez obeyed the fatal logic of borderland honor.

Violence and Authority

Even in the days when the law was ineffective in the borderland, killing to make a point was always defined by the authorities as a crime. At the very least, the authorities always tried to keep track of who was responsible for such killing and stigmatize it as wrong. This was not because they abhorred symbolic violence, however, as can be clearly seen in the account of a young murderer, Ventura Almeida, about to be executed in Cerro Largo in 1883. A sympathetic reporter described his face as bronze and beardless, with penetrating green eyes and an expression of studied humility. He seemed about twenty, but did not know his age. "Do you understand the magnitude of this crime?" the reporter asked. "Today I do," he replied, "but when I committed it, I did not know it was a crime. I thought that killing a person was like slaughtering a cow or a lamb." His explanation was taken seriously by certain townspeople, but they failed to win him clemency. The boy was taken out of town to the isolated spot where he had butchered a woman and child, and there he was tied in a chair, shot by a firing squad, and buried beside his victims. A number of spectators rode out to watch. Obviously, the authorities' purpose in taking Almeida to die humiliatingly in a chair and be buried on the site of his murder was not simply to punish the offense, but also to symbolize the retribution.

The modern state reserves to itself a monopoly on the exercise of violence in society. This exercise is one of its most essential functions, and it puts the authorities directly at odds with the principles of masculine honor based on the capacity to use violence. When a borderland male resorted to his facón to establish or maintain a place for himself in frontier society, he had to deal with the official definition of his act as criminal.

In spite of the ease of mobility and the nearness of the border, men who had been involved in a knife fight rarely forfeited the place they had fought to defend by leaving their homes to escape the law. The Indian boy José went no farther at first than the house of another agregado on the same estancia where he had lived with the murdered man. Bueno loudly told a man who arrived to find Dias's mangled body in front of the pulpería that he had killed him and "there was nothing wrong with it." In the expanses of open frontier, with the law literally days away, Bueno was still captured, and as a result, sentenced to life at hard labor. Arvigo proudly turned himself in, confident of his relationship with the military commander. The saber-carrying stranger Acosta, who seems to have been Brazilian, simply proceeded on his way. Videla claimed self-defense.

The borderlanders' urge to affirm the propriety of their use of symbolic violence can be detected most clearly in frequent, aggressive protestations of scorn for the authorities expected to condemn their actions. In 1832, a young tough belonging to an unfortunate branch of a well-off family in the Brazilian borderland was wanted

(*left*) A mounted beggar wearing the required police license around his neck, 1820s. (Unless cited otherwise, all illustrations are from the Archivo General de la Nación, Buenos Aires, Argentina.)

(*right*) Alcalde de Barrio in Buenos Aires, 1790.

(*bottom*) The three assassins of Facundo Quiroga were shot by a firing squad and then displayed in front of the cabildo in Buenos Aires. (Bonifacio del Carril and Anibal G. Aguirre Saravia, *Iconografía de Buenos Aires. La ciudad de Garay hasta 1852*, Municipalidad de la Ciudad de Buenos Aires, 1982).

Scene from a rural pulpería. As was common, the pulpero is separated from his customers by heavy iron bars.

Gauchos watch a cock fight in a rural pulpería.

(*top left*) Early photograph of rural workers relaxing in front of pulpería. Peon on the left drinks aguardiente while woman on the right prepares yerba mate.

(*bottom left*) Three police sergeants, 1890. The group reflects the breadth of the Federal Police recruitment pool, with a criollo on the left, a European in the middle, and a black on the right.

(*above*) Buenos Aires policeman on right and fireman, 1899.

(*top left*) Police carry victim from scene of labor violence, 1900.

(*bottom left*) Arrest made on the street in Buenos Aires, 1901.

(*above*) Paddy wagon delivers prisoner to jail, 1906.

(*top left*) Armed sailor orders striker off the docks, 1907.

(*bottom left*) Striking railway workers seize a train at the Lanus station, 1912.

(*above*) Capture of a gang of encendiaries and cattle thieves that had terrorized Arrecifes. The police photographer numbered the criminals. Number 5, identified as Urcuti, was seriously wounded in the fight with police, 1920.

(*above*) Police bicycle unit, 1921.

(*top right*) Two "homeless and undernourished" children awaiting transfer to the orphanage, 1923.

(*bottom right*) Police carrying leg-irons used in transporting prisoners sentenced to hard labor in Patagonia, 1925.

(*top*) During the 1920s, the police increasingly used trucks and cars to enhance mobility.

Police arrest ticket scalper outside Club Hurracán, 1929.

(*top*) Two armed robbers wounded while resisting arrest are delivered to the hospital, 1930.

Detectives break up an illegal still, 1930.

(*top*) Handcuffed prisoner delivered to prison by Federal Police, 1934.

Two suspects frisked by police officers in downtown Buenos Aires, 1930.

Illustration from training text showing proper form for directing traffic, 1937.

Magazines offering a mix of photographs of night club performers and soft pornography were designed to attract clients to the Buenos Aires' red light district. (*Vida Nocturna*, Buenos Aires, 17 de diciembre de 1929.)

for murder. Traveling north to the administrative center of Cachoeira, he rode his horse through the door of a pulpería, bragged of
the killing, and pronounced himself so well armed that he had no
reason to fear the authorities. He told the town's Indian goldsmith
that he was inclined to put a bullet through the door of the justice
of the peace, just for good measure.[26] More than half a century
later on the other side of the border, Ventura Royano, a twenty-
eight-year-old soldier of the Uruguayan 4th Cavalry whose father
had an estancia nearby, was in the pulpería telling of his exploits.
One of the other men, Luis Moreyra, gave Royano a shove, pulled
his facón, and doubted publicly that the young soldier was really
"more man than the others." Wrapping his poncho around his
left forearm, Royano drew his facón and met the challenge. The
two circled and slashed until Moreyra fell with a gash in the neck.
The defeated man had to keep still in order not to bleed to death.
He would carry a visible scar to commemorate Royano's prowess.
The young victor had a fine moment in the presence of several
men of his father's estancia. He loudly dared the Brazilian pulpero
to call the authorities. The son of Lieutenant Colonel Royano feared
no man.[27]

Conclusions

Knife duels in pulperías are only one manifestation of general
patterns of thought common in many of the world's cultures, but
often quite perplexing to those unacquainted with them. Several
points about these duels are clear. First, pulpería violence was symbolic. The attacker hoped to show something about himself rather
than simply destroy his opponent, which seldom served any useful end. The violence was expressive rather than instrumental. Further, the violence expressed something only when viewed as a part
of a certain scheme of social psychology, the system of honor. Men
lived prescribed roles as best they could, and their honor, adjudi-
cated by the group, was a measure of how well they succeeded.
The role of each person was dependent upon the group to which
he belonged, and the gaucho culture included competition with
knives. Finally, the system of honor was by no means the only
determinant of these men's behavior. Class and race distinctions
were ever present. They shaped perceptions of relations between

individuals, as when a white man presumed to saberwhip his Indian hired hand, and also affected those relations materially, as when solicitous onlookers saved a man of good family.

The startled young protagonist of W. H. Hudson's *The Purple Land that England Lost* preferred to leave the estancia when he was informed that he should kill someone as soon as possible. The attitude of the men who explained this situation to him seemed mystifying at best, but it is no longer. Richard was attacked initially as a test. His success in the knife fight made him a candidate for a place in a masculine community where hierarchy was based on skill with a facón. Suddenly accepting him, the men of the estancia told him to forget the authorities and prepare himself for further tests, which would continue until he established his place decisively by killing a man. At the end of the book, Hudson appeals to his English readers to comprehend the fierce and archaic life of the Banda Oriental. Gazing out from a high hill before boarding the ship that will take him away, the protagonist Richard realizes that to make sense of his experiences in nineteenth-century South America, he must divest himself of his "English spectacles."[28]

Notes

1. W. H. Hudson, *The Purple Land that England Lost: Travels and Adventures in the Banda Oriental, South America*, 2 vols. (London, 1885). Though fictionalized, *The Purple Land* reveals Hudson's detailed knowledge of the time, place, and people. On Hudson's life, see Ruth Tomalin, *W. H. Hudson: A Biography* (London, 1982).

For a social history of "progress" in nineteenth-century Buenos Aires province, see Richard W. Slatta, *Gauchos and the Vanishing Frontier* (Lincoln, 1983). Silvio R. Duncan Baretta and John Markoff also provide a hemispheric overview with particular attention to violence in "Civilization and Barbarism: Cattle Frontiers in Latin America," *Comparative Studies in Society and History* (Oct. 1978).

2. Hudson, *the Purple Land*, 1: 94–99.

3. For background on Rio Grande do Sul, see Joseph L. Love, *Rio Grande do Sul and Brazilian Regionalism, 1882–1930* (Stanford, 1971), pp. 3–25; and the novel by Erico Veríssimo, *Time and the Wind*, trans. L. L. Barrett (New York, 1951), which depicts a knife duel on pp. 217–19.

4. See Rhys Isaac's scheme of cultural interpretation from historical descriptions of behavior in *The Transformation of Virginia, 1740–1790* (Chapel

Hill, N.C., 1982), pp. 323–57, an appendix entitled "A Discourse on the Method: Action, Structure, and Meaning."

5. The pulpería was an important feature of rural life. This recreation of a typical interior is taken from Alcides Maya, *Ruinas vivas* (Porto, 1910), pp. 59–61.

6. Brazilian court records are identified by município, year, category, case number, bundle number, and shelf number: Arquivo Público do Rio Grande do Sul (hereinafter APRGS), Município de Cachoeira 1829/Crime 2850–1–56.

7. APRGS, Cachoeira 1831/Crime 2854–1–56.

8. This and other aspects of violence as a structure of community are noted by Baretta and Markoff in "Civilization and Barbarism," pp. 612–15.

9. Captured three years later, Bueno was condemned to life at hard labor, but capture, conviction, and punishment was the exception rather than the rule.

10. Robert Crawford, *South American Sketches* (London, 1898), pp. 41–42.

11. Archivo General de la Nación (hereinafter AGN), Montevideo, Sección Judicial-Juzgado Letrado de Cerro Largo (hereinafter AGNJ-CLL) 1863/case 32. (Uruguayan judicial archives are organized by court, department, year, and a single index number. All Uruguayan cases cited here are from the Juzgado Letrado of Cerro Largo, so that the distinctive part of each citation is the year and index number.) The second case is AGNJ-CLL 1860/7.

12. Statistics are from: 1) "Causas criminales," from the yearly report of the police chief of Tacuarembó, 1867; AGN, Jefaturas de Policía, Carlos Reiles to Ministerio de Gobierno, Jan. 1868, addendum 2; 2) "Relación de muertes violentas," *Memoria de la Jefatura Política y de Policía del Departamento de Cerro Largo correspondiente a los años de 1876–1877–1878* (Montevideo, 1879), addendum 29; 3) *Anuario estadístico de la República Oriental del Uruguay* (Montevideo, 1886), pp. 458–59; and 4) AHRGS, *Relatório do Presidente da Província*, Francisco Xavier Pinto Lima, delivered 14 Mar. 1871, pp. 4–6.

13. The judge, Ramón Montero, gave the wounded Naranjo two days to leave Melo; AGNJ-CLL 1838/12.

14. Acosta, a Brazilian, simply crossed the border and was never questioned; AGN-CLL 1869/6.

15. A detailed study of the system of honor in Hispanic society is available in Julian Pitt-Rivers, *The Fate of Shechem or the Politics of Sex: Essays in the Anthropology of the Mediterranean* (Cambridge, 1977). For recent historical studies employing the concept, see Ramón A. Gutiérrez, "From Honor to Love: Transformations of the Meaning of Sexuality in Colonial New Mexico," in *Kinship Ideology and Practice in Latin America*, ed. Ramond

T. Smith (Chapel Hill, N.C., 1984) and Bertram Wyatt-Brown, *Southern Honor: Ethics and Behavior in the Old South* (Oxford, 1982).

16. AGNJ-CLL 1861/14. Two Portuguese shopkeepers brawl in Brazil: APRGS Piratini 1833/Crime 1067–25–14. Two Spanish shopkeepers fight each other over a question of honor in Uruguay: AGNJ-CLL 1858/8. An Irish ditchdigger kills his English partner; AGNJ-CLL 1859/4. Two feuding Spanish farmers pelt each other with rocks and lawsuits: AGN-CLL 1893/105.

17. "Contestación," *El Deber Cívico*, 31 July 1894.

18. Though in Hispanic law a man's honor has a legal status that it does not have in Anglo-Saxon law, the two principles of ethics remain basically at odds. Pitt-Rivers elaborates on this idea in "Honor," *International Encyclopedia of the Social Sciences*, p. 509.

19. Augustin Saint-Hilaire, *Voyage à Rio-Grande do Sul (Brésil)* (Orléans, 1887), p. 252.

20. Though the word *gaucho* at first described drifters, mostly of mixed or Indian blood, by the latter part of the nineteenth century it meant any uneducated country man with the customs and preoccupations of estancia life; Roberto J. Bouton, *La vida rural en el Uruguay* (Montevideo, 1961), pp. 41–44.

21. From the probate inventory done at the death of his wife, Propicia de la Rosa; AGNJ-CLL 1880/167.

22. Nepomuceno Saravia García, *Memorias de Aparicio Saravia* (Montevideo, 1956), pp. 19–23.

23. AGNJ-CLL 1839/22.

24. Of course, the richest of the landowners towered above all the rest with 203,020 pesos. Computed from AGN, Departamento de Cerro Largo, Fondo Ex Archivo General Administrativo, Libro 659, "Declaración de Contribuyentes, 1860."

25. AGNJ-CLL 1869/87.

26. The young man's name was Abel Pereira da Luz; APRGS, Cachoeira 1832/Crime 2861–1–56.

27. The judge thought this was a case of self-defense; AGN-CLL 1893/106.

28. Hudson, *The Purple Land*, 2: 235–46.

4

Urbanization, Crime, and Policing

Buenos Aires, 1880–1914

Julia Kirk Blackwelder

Historians of urbanization in the Western world have observed that crime rates and police practices showed remarkably similar patterns in the industrial cities of the West from the late nineteenth through the early twentieth centuries. This was especially true for cities in the United States. From these observations, students of crime concluded that the very process of urban growth during the industrial age created a rather predictable cycle of criminal activity and police behavior. Because of the similarity between the growth of Buenos Aires and cities of the United States, a comparison of criminal patterns and police behaviors in these different environments highlights the deficiencies of invoking urbanization alone as an explanation for these phenomena.[1]

North American cities that grew rapidly before their industrial bases matured were raucous and disorderly places in which respectable citizens demanded and obtained the establishment of a professional police force to restore order and keep daily life running as smoothly as possible. As the industrial order impinged directly on more and more individual lives, urban residents settled down to the quieter life styles that reflected the discipline of the factory or office.[2] Initially, the police enforced public order on the industrializing city by arresting persons who exhibited drunken or otherwise disorderly behavior in public places, but eventually the demands of employers and the discipline of urban social institutions such as the church and school partly replaced the police as agents of social control.[3]

As the industrial city matured, it grew more orderly, but other social problems increased. Conspicuous consumption, material differences between social classes, and anonymity also grew. Both the concentration of wealth and the display of wealth in industrial cities offered previously unknown opportunities for thievery, robbery, embezzlement, and other crimes against property. Urban citizens shifted their concerns from social disorder to property crime and demanded that police similarly redirect their priorities. By the early twentieth century, police in North American cities had succeeded in bringing a high proportion of these offenders before the judge's bench. Effective policing, a rising standard of living, and increased respect for the rights of private property all contributed to an overall decrease in crime as the process of industrialization was completed in the United States. On the eve of World War I, most cities in the United States were orderly, persons were relatively safe on the streets, and property was as secure from theft as it has ever been before or since. Exceptions were places such as metropolitan San Francisco, where frontier conditions remained despite its long history and where an earthquake destroyed any semblance of order or normal life.[4]

While historians have never claimed that this cycle of disorder and crime applied to the non-Western world, similar patterns have been cited in Western cities that experienced generally contemporaneous patterns of urban growth and industrialization. The history of crime and policing in Buenos Aires during this same period of rapid population growth and commercial and industrial development reveals that political and cultural influences are as important as economic development in determining patterns of crime and the relative effectiveness of the police in coping with citizens' demands for order and security. Conversely, there are marked similarities between criminal patterns in Buenos Aires and North American cities. An initial period of perceived disorder followed by a later period of increased social order, but high rates of property crime, characterized rapidly industrializing cities outside as well as within the United States during these years.[5]

The rapid population growth that occurred in Buenos Aires between 1870 and World War I paralleled the growth of cities in the Northeastern and Midwestern United States. All these cities experienced population increases, mostly because of European immigration, but the sources of immigration to Argentina were substantially different from U.S. countries of origin. Eastern and Southern Europe were especially important sources for the United States after the turn of the century, but the highest proportion of foreign-born residents in American cities came from the British Isles, with smaller numbers coming from Western Europe. Although Argentina also received immigrants from all these areas, Italy and Spain were the leading sources of Argentine immigration in the late nineteenth and early twentieth centuries. Italian immigration to the United States was also heavy, and in fact numerically greater than Italian immigration to Argentina, but Spanish immigration to the United States has been small in comparison with immigration to the Spanish-speaking countries of the Western Hemisphere. For Argentina and Buenos Aires, the immigration of the late nineteenth and early twentieth centuries had a more profound impact on the composition of the total population than the arrival of foreigners had on the population of the United States. In 1910, roughly 15 percent of U.S. residents were foreign-born, while in Argentina the foreign-born accounted for roughly 30 percent of the total population.

In Buenos Aires, Boston, Chicago, New York, Philadelphia, and other American cities, immigrant populations comprised islands of national or regional cultures within a foreign context. Those many and varied ethnic cultures created a unique urban environment in each city.[6] Culturally, no two cities in the United States were alike, and none replicated the context of Buenos Aires. In studying urbanization, however, the "new" urban historians have focused largely on process rather than on the influence of distinctive cultures. A recent book by Roger Lane has boldly confronted the significance of ethnic differences in social behavior, demonstrating that the process of migration and urban growth do not totally explain patterns of crime, disorder, and policing in the city.[7] The case of Buenos Aires presents an opportunity to see crime not only in an ethnic setting very different from that of North American cities, but also to examine disorder, crime, and policing in a city with patterns of governance that differed from the machine-dominated cities of the United States.[8]

In the cities of the Northeastern and Midwestern United States, immigration aggravated the overcrowding and deterioration of the urban environment to which internal migration and natural population increase also contributed. The same situation prevailed in Buenos Aires during these years of rapid growth. In both the United States and Argentina, foreign tongues were heard much more frequently in the city than in small towns or in the countryside, because immigrants remained disproportionately in urban areas. In both countries, nativists identified immigrants as an important, if not the major, cause of urban problems, including crime, disease, and disorder. In Buenos Aires and in the cities of the United States between 1880 and World War I, civic leaders demanded that city governments take action to clean up the cities, "restore" the supposed order of an earlier age, and protect the substantial property holdings of the middle and upper classes. In 1880, the government of Buenos Aires was in a better position to try to control its population than were some North American cities. In 1880, Buenos Aires employed seventy-six police officers for every ten thousand residents as opposed to fourteen officers per ten thousand population in New Haven, Connecticut, and twenty officers in Boston, Massachusetts. Arrest rates in Buenos Aires reflected the superior size of its police force. In 1880, the arrest rate in Buenos Aires was more than twice as high as in New Haven or Boston.[9]

During the late nineteenth and early twentieth centuries, Buenos Aires expanded in a fashion that paralleled growth in North American cities. During the nineteenth century, industrialists and commercial agents in the United States actively encouraged immigration from abroad. Although the Chinese Exclusion Act of 1886 and the Gentlemen's Agreement of 1905 had effectively terminated immigration from Asia, the federal government encouraged immigration from Europe until the 1920s. The government of Argentina similarly encouraged immigration from Europe with the hope that the newcomers would pursue agricultural work in the nation's virgin interior. Although Buenos Aires proved highly attractive to migrant Europeans, however, the Argentine hinterlands did not. As was also true in the United States, immigrants to Argentina in this period lacked the financial resources to invest immediately in property, and most arrived with no money or only enough to provide for their upkeep for a short period. Employment at the point of debarkation was the first priority for immigrants who did not already have family living elsewhere in the new country.

Buenos Aires, like the cities of North America, could not immediately assimilate the vast, new populations who brought virtually no economic resources with them. Immigrants settled for casual labor when they could find it and pooled their resources to rent housing in rapidly declining residential areas. The combination of low earnings and high housing demand inevitably led to tenement expansion in city after city where this process occurred. From 1880 until World War I, the tenement, or *conventillo*, districts of Buenos Aires continued to expand at the same time that they became more overcrowded and the housing stock deteriorated. From 1883 to 1890, population density in the *conventillos* increased from 35 to 42 persons per structure.[10] In the center city, population density continued to increase until World War I.

As immigration and other sources of population growth swelled the city's size and exacerbated the overcrowding and the deterioration of the inner city, well-to-do citizens fled to the outskirts. Elite suburbs developed on the north side of the city. In this process of suburbanization, the elite adopted the architectural styles that maximized the gardenlike settings of their new homes. Forsaking the walled enclosures and courtyard focus of the Spanish colonial style, the suburbanites built homes with doors and large windows that faced the streets. In Buenos Aires as in North American cities, architectural styles made uninvited entrance to private residences easier at the same time that the often-ostentacious display of wealth made theft and burglary more tempting.[11]

Buenos Aires developed turn-of-the-century suburbs partly because horse-drawn streetcars and eventually electric trollies made it practical for all but the poorest urban residents to live outside the commercial or manufacturing centers where they worked and shopped. Streetcars in Buenos Aires, as in other cities of Europe and America, encouraged the residential segregation of economic classes. Generally speaking, the wealth of neighborhoods increased as their distance from the center city grew. Older residential stock and outdated commercial buildings at the waterfront or at the heart of the city became the housing of the poor. With the withdrawal of the middle and upper classes from these residential zones, deterioration and overcrowding mounted. Simultaneously, public demand for neighborhood order and personal safety diminished in the central city.

Closeted in their comfortable, conspicuous, and vulnerable garden-homes, the middle and upper classes, who controlled politics and the press, demanded that the police protect their interests. In most cities, some of the wealthier citizens hired private security personnel to protect their business and residential properties, while they also expected the municipal police to make their interests a priority. Suburban areas consequently received proportionally more police protection than the congested urban areas, and the ability of the police to patrol areas of high population density was thereby diminished. The spending patterns and lifestyles of the affluent made them especially vulnerable to crimes that the poor were unlikely to suffer and police patrols could not supress. Employee theft was common in Buenos Aires. Servants who had been convicted of theft from their employers led the ranks of women committed to the penitentiary in Buenos Aires.[12]

In contrast to persons of property, the poorest urban residents owned little and had few means to protect their meager possessions. Their homes, rooms they shared with persons other than immediate-family members, offered the poor neither privacy nor respite from worldly cares. Cramped and unpleasant, home was a place to avoid as the poor sought recreation or social pleasures. Children were not isolated from the adult world and moved freely from home to street. For the urban poor of the early twentieth century, as for the inner-city underclasses of today, commerce occurred in the streets as well as in stores. Socializing and recreation took place in saloons or in the streets and were not limited to homes, parks, and gardens. Under such circumstances, the functions of urban institutions became confused. A saloon might have been both a center for community organizing and an arena for settling interpersonal differences. In such contexts, recreation and social intercourse easily led to public disorder.

The available data on crime indicate that personal safety and public order in Buenos Aires changed considerably between 1880 and World War I. Public-order arrests crested in 1885, when there were 28,447 arrests for public drunkenness and 15,115 arrests for public disturbances in this city of 395,000 people, or 1 arrest for every 9 residents. Arrests for order violations mounted swiftly during the late 1880s, but then declined precipitously until the politically troubled early teens. In 1913, there were 55,330 order arrests as opposed to a low of roughly 25,000 arrests in 1903 and 1904. On the basis of rates, the twentieth-century arrests were consistently low, however, with approximately 1 arrest for every 40 persons in 1904 and 1 for every 28 persons in 1913.[13]

In contrast, crimes against persons or property either were not usually reported or occurred at very low rates by modern standards. In 1885, 1 crime was reported annually for every 247 residents of Buenos Aires. The trend in the data of crimes reported to the police was distinctly different from the pattern of order arrests. The numbers of crimes against persons and property reported to the police rose steadily but gradually until 1901, when property crime declined slightly. Crimes against persons declined substantially in 1903. By 1907, crimes against persons and against property had both increased numerically again. In 1913, the police recorded a total of 14,026 crimes against persons or property, or 1 incident for every 111 persons. Judging by these indicators of crime and disorder, a person who lived in Buenos Aires on the eve of World War I was much less likely to be frightened or harassed by unseemly displays of public behavior than he would have been twenty years earlier, but he was twice as likely to be the victim of a crime against his property or person. Buenos Aires, like most North American cities, appeared to be a better-ordered city in the early twentieth century than it had been in the late nineteenth century. Unlike the citizens of most U.S. cities, however, the residents of the Argentine capital did not experience an increase in personal safety as World War I approached.

Although the rate of crimes reported to the police in Buenos Aires rose between the 1880s and World War I, one indicator of serious crime held steady. Homicide rates fluctuated during these years, but the variations were small, and no long-term increase or decrease occurred. As historian Roger Lane has argued, homicide rates are among the most accurate criminal statistics available, because bureaucracies regularly certify all deaths, and evidence of foul play is not easily disguised.[14] The homicide rate in Buenos Aires remained approximately 1 incident per 10,000 population during these years. By way of contrast, homicide rates in North American cities declined from the late ninteenth century until the second decade of the twentieth century.[15]

Rates of reported assaults are not as reliable as homicide statistics, but these figures also suggest that Buenos Aires did not become either more or less dangerous as the city grew or as immigration increased. Assault rates were at their lowest in the 1880s and their highest between 1897 and 1901. While crimes against persons occurred at a generally stable rate, the reports of crimes against property exhibited a definite upward trend over the period, although they fluctuated significantly in the short term. In 1885, there were 25 reported property offenses for every 10,000 persons in the city. By 1915, the rate had risen to 58 per 10,000. Clearly, personal security did not decline as the city grew, but the security of property did. From the late nineteenth century until 1900, U.S. cities appeared to demonstrate a decrease in all crimes with victims.[16] The conclusion that crime was diminishing, however, is based on arrests rather than crime reports, and the U.S. figures do not separate crimes against persons from crimes against property.

The increase in criminal activity that occurred in Buenos Aires as the city grew and modernized did not necessarily represent the disintegration of older moral values that had previously suppressed theft and personal violence. The rise in reported crimes probably occurred because of increasing incentives produced by economic crises and more opportunities to commit property crimes, as poverty-stricken individuals crowded into commercial areas and gained access to private residences. The apparent crime rate also would have risen as the habit of filing reports with the police became established.

In the short run, the pattern of the increase in reported crimes followed economic indicators in Buenos Aires. The city suffered four recessions from the 1880s until World War I. During each of these periods of general economic hardship, the number of crimes reported to the police rose. As would be expected, the incidence of crimes against property was much more sensitive to economic conditions than was the rate of crimes against persons. Outside this pattern of periodic fluctuation, however, the distinct trend of an increase in serious crime remains. The economic development of the city was in itself an incentive to commit crime. Homes and shops of the industrial-age city flaunted material wealth, and great disparities of wealth became increasingly evident when measured in consumer goods. In Buenos Aires, burglars and thieves faced lower risks of retribution as urbanization progressed. From the 1880s until World War I, the effectiveness of the police in clearing crimes by arrest steadily declined. During the 1880s and 1890s, the share of crimes cleared by arrest fluctuated between 54 and 74 percent. For the first decade of the twentieth century, the share remained below 55 percent, and for the second decade, it declined below 50 percent. Both the pattern of crime and the effectiveness of the police in Buenos Aires contrast with the situation in North American cities during these same years of rapid urbanization.[17]

In Buenos Aires at the turn of the century, a few observers noted the congestion, confusion, and deteriorating conditions of the central city and blamed the new immigrants for the situation. Argentines did not merely associate crime and disorder with immigration because of the concentration of newcomers in deplorable slums. The police department of Buenos Aires collected and regularly reported arrest statistics by national origin. These statistics were published annually in yearbooks compiled and printed by the municipality of Buenos Aires. From the 1880s until World War I, the arrest statistics for males conveyed two messages very clearly to the casual observer. Most arrests were for public drunkenness or disturbing the peace, and most were of persons judged by the police not to be of Argentine origin. Buenos Aires appeared to be a city struggling to maintain order in the face of a wave of uncivilized immigrants.

The press of Buenos Aires and other local voices decried the rise in crime and disorder during these years. In Argentina as in the United States, criminology emerged as a field of academic inquiry. Monographs on crime and escalating concern for public safety evoked demands for penal and police reform, which also occurred in U.S. cities during the Progressive Era. In Argentina, contemporary works on crime included *Problemas de criminalidad*, which was written by Norberto Pinero and published in 1888. Eusebio Gómez's *El problema penal argentino* and M. A. Lancelotti's *La criminalidad en Buenos Aires* both appeared in 1912. All these works cited immigrants as a criminal element.[18] By 1910, the municipal government had recognized a link between the immigrant population and crime and disorder in Buenos Aires. In that year, the city published Roberto Levillier's essay on crime as an introduction to the criminal-statistics section of the 1909 census of Buenos Aires. Levillier minced no words in blaming the city's problems not simply on the immigrants, but particularly on the indolent and depraved habits of the newcomers, rather than the desperateness of their conditions. Levillier told his readers that "Buenos Aires has scarcely room for the avalanche of immigrants who prefer remaining in the city to working in the country. They live in the city, though with difficulty; from that to discontent and a desire to obtain with a minimum of effort what cannot be obtained by labor, is but a step: hence theft in various forms."[19] Lest there be any doubt as to the state to which immigrant populations had fallen, Levillier claimed to know that "more than 50 percent of the criminals of different nationalities, especially Spaniards and Italians, are alcoholic degenerates, and many others are habitual drunkards." Levillier endorsed legislation to "prevent the arrival of dangerous and undesirable persons" as being "another step toward diminishing crime in Buenos Aires."

Evidently, many of these dangerous immigrants were entering the country as children, because Levillier also argued that most adult offenders had begun their march to the penitentiary as juvenile delinquents. Social commentators and reformers throughout the world have always regarded city streets as the breeding ground of juvenile crime. Levillier believed that children who roamed the streets of Buenos Aires were a danger to society and to themselves. Although juvenile law in Argentina had not developed to the extent that it had in Western Europe and the United States, both national and local regulations gave the courts potential control over the city's children. An 1886 law empowered city courts to act in loco parentis for the "protection, education, and professional instruction" of runaway and abandoned children.[20] Apparently the courts did not discharge these responsibilities, for in 1905, the director of the boys' reformatory recommended that all boys who had completed sentences at the reformatory and who were "morally or materially abandoned" should be sent to a rural boys' colony. Otherwise, they would surely return to the life that had landed them in the reformatory originally. A presidential degree instituting the director's recommendation was in effect from 1905 through August of 1906, when it was declared illegal by the federal Court of Appeal. In 1900, Argentina instituted compulsory school attendance, a policy that likewise went unenforced in Buenos Aires. The existence of these laws and the failure to enforce them were common situations in Western cities at the turn of the century, but criminologist Roberto Levillier believed that the consequences of neglect were more serious in Buenos Aires than elsewhere. Levillier claimed that juvenile crime was more prevalent in Buenos Aires than elsewhere and that most adult criminals, whether immigrant or native-born, had honed their skills as children of the streets.

The Buenos Aires data clearly demonstrate that immigrants accounted for most of the arrests for serious crimes during the period. In 1913, when approximately half the city's population were native-born persons, Argentines accounted for 32 percent of those arrested for crimes against person or property. In individual years from 1882 through 1913, Argentines accounted for anywhere from 32 to 44 percent of total arrests. In contrast, Spanish and Italian immigrants comprised between 42 and 55 percent of arrested persons, with other national groups accounting for the remainder of the arrests in each year. Immigrants were also those most frequently arrested for public drunkenness or disorderly behavior.

Police acted similarly in the cities of the United States that were transformed by immigration, and interethnic hostilities have contributed to urban violence in the United States from the 1830s to the present. A recent study of crime in Alameda County, California, from 1870 to 1910 shows a pattern of immigrant harassment similar to that occurring in Buenos Aires during these years. Immigrants appeared on the police blotter more frequently than the native-born in Oakland, the county's largest city, and the police calculated initiative arrests from their own biases. The Irish had an overall arrest rate three times that of the native-born. The Chinese in Oakland were despised by the city's whites, and in 1875, an Oakland newspaper reported the arrest of an individual "on suspicion of being a Chinaman."[21] Overall, the Chinese were unlikely to experience arrest for public-order violations, because they remained cloistered in Chinatown, where they did not regularly confront the white citizenry. After an 1876 riot in Chinatown in which many were reportedly injured, the city made no arrests. The Chinese in Oakland, however, were disproportionately arrested for reported crimes that stemmed from their commercial exchanges with whites, such as the failure to observe specific business codes.

Although the average citizen of Buenos Aires or Oakland might have concluded from the arrest data that immigrants endangered the safety of local residents, to do so overlooked the possibility that the police made arrests selectively. Police departments set priorities in terms of the numbers of patrolmen in specific locations and types of criminal offenses they identify as most troublesome. At the bureaucratic level and on the beat, policemen may target particular populations as suspicious. Given the possible nativism of the police and the condemnation of immigrants in the press and other publications, immigrants were undoubtedly special targets for arrest.

Amidst concern about an immigrant crime wave in Buenos Aires, one observer attempted to analyze the situation objectively and present an alternative interpretation of arrest statistics. While avoiding the question of the role of police prejudice in making arrests, criminologist M. A. Lancelotti pointed out that demographic differences between the immigrant and native-born populations could account for the higher arrest rate among immigrants than among the native-born.[22] In his 1912 monograph, Lancelotti argued that the peculiar age distribution of immigrant groups distorted their arrest rates in comparison with the native-born. Lancelotti found that, when he calculated arrest rates for native-born Argentines on the basis of the population aged fifteen through seventy years, the rate for Argentines roughly equaled that of other national groups.

Had Lancelotti refined the level of his analysis further, he could have produced a more convincing argument that immigrants were not particularly crime-prone and that the much-feared Spaniards and Italians had been unjustly maligned. Historians and criminologists agree that males between the ages of sixteen and fifty years of age committed the majority of crimes in urban settings during the years in question. Arrest rates calculated on this select population (see Table 1) yield a different picture of crime in Buenos Aires than either the press or Lancelotti portrayed.

Immigrants were indeed much more likely to be arrested than the native-born, but the greatest difference between Argentines and newcomers was their likelihood of arrest for an order violation, which relied almost wholly on police initiative and represented a minor infraction. In the area of serious criminal offenses, Argentines were as likely to enter the justice system as were Italians and more likely than were French immigrants. The highest arrest rates for order offenses occurred among the British, who, because of their relatively small presence in the city, had not been singled out by the press as a dangerous group. The extremely high arrest rates among the British probably reflected the presence of British sailors on leave in the Argentine port city. Overall, the most "dangerous" ethnic group seems to have been Argentina's neighbors, the Uruguayans.[23] These laborers may have traveled to Buenos

Table 1
Arrest Rates per 1,000 Males Aged 16–50 by Nationality, 1910*

Nationality	Public drunkenness (N per 1,000)	Public disturbances (N per 1,000)	Criminal offenses (N per 1,000)
Argentines	27.7	28.7	13.5
Italians	33.9	30.5	13.1
Spaniards	59.3	50.3	19.5
French	75.1	76.9	11.4
British	172.7	98.6	15.3
Uruguayans	72.9	88.5	33.2

*The arrest data do not discriminate between resident aliens and transients passing through the port.
Sources: Rates are computed using arrests in 1909 and population data from City of Buenos Aires, *Censo General de Población, Edificación, Comercio e Industrias, 1909*, 3 vols. (Buenos Aires, 1910).

Aires as Uruguayan nationals in search of work. Already branded by the Argentine government as undesirable, such newcomers may have been an especially desperate and troublesome lot whom authorities sought to harass or to deport.

The focus of contemporary observers on the supposed criminal tendencies of immigrants caused them to overlook some obvious socioeconomic characteristics of those arrested. During the early twentieth century, day laborers accounted for nine of every ten people arrested for drunkenness or disorderly behavior and eight of every ten indicted for criminal offenses, while they accounted for one in ten or two in ten of the city's work force during these years. Most crimes in Buenos Aires were committed by men who had failed to achieve a dependable level of wage earning or enter the better-paying trades. Economic status was a more accurate single predictor of arrest than ethnicity. Although Levillier paid special attention to the foreign-born in analyzing male criminal patterns in the city, he concluded that among women "it is those with no trade who commit most crimes."[24] Levillier thus acknowledged that poverty or the inability to earn steady wages encouraged social deviance among women, while he blamed ethnic characteristics, rather than their marginal economic status, for similar behaviors by men.

The inability of the Buenos Aires police to clear crimes by arrest further suggests that their primary goals were to discipline population groups they regarded as troublesome or undesirable. In comparison with the police in North American cities, the police in Buenos Aires were ineffective in apprehending offenders. This may partly reflect the increasing burdens placed upon them. Traffic control required more police power in the early twentieth-century city than it had earlier and such activities may have caused the number of arrests per officer to decline in Boston and New Haven.[25] The efficiency of the police in Buenos Aires, however, had declined much more precipitously around the turn of the century than it had in the two North American cities. Contemporary U.S. experience reveals that police are less apt to clear crimes by arrest when the ratio of crimes reported to the number of policemen also rises. Clearly, this was the case in Buenos Aires during these years. The number of criminal arrests per officer also declined, though, indicating that the police were becoming less successful in an absolute as well as a relative sense.

A number of circumstances may help explain why the quality of police services declined in Buenos Aires more than it did in the United States. The close connections between police departments and the political machines of many cities had made appointment to the police department highly sought after in cities of the United States. While political corruption discouraged efficient policing, it encouraged growth in the size of departments. As U.S. cities became more orderly and the police developed improved communications, much of the danger went out of police work. During the Progressive Era, procedural and political reforms encouraged police efficiency. Neither of these situations was true in Buenos Aires, and consequently the city had a difficult time recruiting officers. Between 1884 and 1914, sixty-eight police officers in Buenos Aires died in the line of duty. Only nine of these deaths were accidental. Thirty-seven deaths were enforcement related, and fifty deaths resulted from political attacks on the police, uncommon occurrences in the United States despite the 1886 tragedy in Chicago's Haymarket Square. In potentially dangerous labor demonstrations in the United States, private police such as the Pinkerton guards often formed the front ranks who defended commercial properties.[26]

The 1890 Argentine depression provided an important lesson for the police of Buenos Aires. The depression was accompanied by a violent uprising by the *Unión Cívica Radical* and epidemic outbreaks of smallpox and typhus. Desperate circumstances forced immigrants to leave Buenos Aires in such high numbers that a net loss of immigrants was recorded for the first time in the city's history. Reported crimes rose precipitously, but the arrest rate rose even faster. Buenos Aires was coming apart, and the police struggled to hold it together. In the process, the police learned that their effectiveness was strongly related to the visibility of violators and the geographic limits of their activities. As they concentrated on controlling the activities of demonstrators, police confronted a compact range of street behaviors that were easier to monitor than the random actions of individual burglars and thieves. Arrests in the former case involved little detective activity. Arrests could be made as the activities occurred or shortly thereafter. In 1890, the proportion of arrests that were made on the streets reached an all-time high. The following year, the arrest pattern was very different. The number of arrests on the streets remained about the same numerically, but the number of arrests made elsewhere tripled. The year 1891 stands out within the period as one in which the police had determined to institute a crackdown on crime, a drive that evidently succeeded despite the manpower shortage. Police response to the 1890–91 crisis demonstrated that, when the police department perceived an imminent threat to the city, it could respond mightily, but that it was unable to do so without this stimulus. Whether the unusually high arrest rate in 1892 constituted effective policing or police harassment of troublesome residents cannot be known, but the police proved unable to enforce this level of social control thereafter. Arrests dropped precipitously in 1893, and the proportion of crimes not cleared by arrest continued to rise until World War I.

In the case of day-to-day crime, each arrest was most likely preceded by a report to the police and subsequent investigation, both of which increased the perpetrator's chances of escape. In the case of theft, the crime was frequently not observed and consequently might go undetected for a considerable time. Buenos Aires also suffered a recession at the end of the 1890s. Although less severe than the 1890 depression, the downturn at the end of the decade was accompanied by a higher number of crimes reported than during the earlier dislocation. Although the arrest rate rose, it did not reach the 1891 high, and consequently the share of crime cleared by arrest declined. The economic dislocation of the late 1890s did not trigger the popular unrest and protest of the earlier depression. Police were less likely to observe violators in the act of breaking the law than they had been during the 1890–91 protests.

As Buenos Aires grew spatially, the police became a less visible presence on the streets. Their increase in manpower failed to keep pace with geographic expansion and population growth. Police manpower declined from seventy-six officers per ten thousand residents in 1880 to forty-nine officers per ten thousand in 1903. The arrest rate per officer declined from 20 to 6 per year, and the overall arrest rate declined from 156 per 1,000 population to 30 during the same years. The actual decline in police effectiveness did not occur until the beginning of the twentieth century. Although the arrest rate dropped markedly right after the 1890–91 demonstrations, it never returned to the lows of the 1880s. As a measure of police activity, arrest rates indicated that in the matter of criminal arrests (as opposed to order arrests), the police carried on more business after the 1890–91 turning point than they had before. Reports of crimes, though, were rising faster than both the numbers of arrests and the size of the population. Paradoxically, then, police effectiveness was declining at the same time that the arrest rate was rising. With the crime rate rising, police powers were stretched thinner and thinner. As the city grew larger and more complicated, it was easier for identified perpetrators to elude capture. From the 1880s until World War I, the population of the city increased 250 percent, but the size of the police force increased only 20 percent.

Because Buenos Aires did not follow the North American political pattern of tying the police department to a burgeoning and virtually autonomous local political machine, the police force failed to grow with the city. Although the press and civic leaders expressed concern about increasing levels of crime, the financial resources necessary to expand police powers were not appropriated by local officials. Unlike urban administrations in the United States, no parties in the political bureaucracy of Buenos Aires stood to benefit from the expansion of the police department. The shortage of financial means in the police department also had important consequences in the areas of police professionalization and modernization. In 1886, the police opened a training academy, but the training program ended in 1889 because of funding problems. In the late 1880s, the department reported that the low salaries offered to its officers had resulted in eighty vacancies that they were unable to fill locally. The department attempted to fill its vacancies by advertising the positions in interior regions, where prevailing wages were 20 percent lower than in the city.

Confronted by a twenty-year decline in manpower, the police enforced the law selectively. Regressions (see Table 2) of criminal arrests with total crimes reported, with crimes against property and against persons, reveal the superiority of the police in protecting property as opposed to people. The changing arrest rate was as fully explained by property crimes reported as by the combination of property and personal crime. This was not the case for the statistical relationship between the rate of crimes against persons and the arrest rate. Whether the police were more successful in "solving" property crimes than personal crimes, they responded in the form of increased total arrests to a rise in property crime more fully than to a rise in crimes against persons.

When all the problems of inadequate manpower and funding are taken into account, there remains some difficulty in explaining the overall inefficiency of the city's police in comparison with their North American counterparts. The police consistently made fewer arrests per officer than did officers in cities like Boston, Massachusetts, and New Haven, Connecticut.[27] As police in the United States modernized during these years, the number of arrests per officer increased, while it declined in Buenos Aires. Police work, like any other occupation, is partly a matter of motivation. The police in Buenos Aires, especially after the turn of the century, may have lacked the desire to push for improved efficiency. In the United

Table 2
Regression of Criminal Arrest Rates With

(1886–1913)	Pearson's r
Reported crimes against persons	.5057
Reported crimes against property	.7177
Total of reported crimes	.7102

States, police work had become a ladder of social mobility for the lower classes, particularly for immigrants and the children of immigrants.[28] Although wages were not high in absolute terms, they were competitive with many skilled craft positions that had longer periods of apprenticeship and offered fewer chances of advancement. The difficulty in filling police vacancies in Buenos Aires indicates that such circumstances were not the case there. The necessity of obtaining police recruits from the interior is evidence that the police were unwilling to consider applicants from the immigrant underclasses among whom unemployment was consistently high.[29]

In Buenos Aires as in the United States, the growing complexity of urban life accompanied by the development of a distinctly urban social conscience prompted the adoption of many ordinances that regulated urban activities with a view toward making life safer and healthier for all residents. Building codes, sanitation codes, employment regulations, animal-control regulations, and child-welfare laws were all part of this process of urban maturation. As each of these new areas of public control appeared on the statute books, city police departments shouldered the burdens of enforcing local codes.

In the United States, the responsibility for enforcing most public-welfare protection had shifted by World War I to licensing offices outside the police department. In Buenos Aires, where wages were low and officers had little training, the police continued to carry the principal responsibilities for enforcing health and safety regulations. Over the years, the number of arrests made in these areas rose along with criminal arrests. In 1905, the police issued 2,878 citations for violations of codes governing the treatment of animals, housing standards, and the employment of women and children. By 1914, the number of police cases relating to these regulations had risen to 10,975. If such arrests were added to the number of criminal arrests, the overall effectiveness of the police would be greatly enhanced.

In the early part of the twentieth century, the police of Buenos Aires also assumed additional responsibilities not widely borne by North American police departments. They became the official protectors of the federal capital's many public buildings and functioned as a militia on call at all times. The obligation to keep policemen on duty at public buildings on a regular basis further limited both the patrol and detective capacities of the police. The multiplication of tasks, the unavailability of the most modern police technology, the absence of thorough training, and low pay all contributed to the comparative ineffectiveness of the police. Their efficiency was likely to be highest when criminal activities were concentrated in a particular time and place and lowest in relatively tranquil times, when the hard work of detection preceded most arrests. Although Buenos Aires adopted some modern police methods, the changes did not result in more clearing of reported crimes by arrests.[30]

Buenos Aires grew apace with North American cities during the age of industry. In the United States and Argentina, immigration was crucial to urban expansion, although the nationalities of the newcomers differed from place to place. Arrests for drunken and disorderly behavior were very high among immigrants, but the arrest rates differed by nationality among immigrants to Argentina. The differing arrest rates demonstrated both the generally poor living conditions among the immigrants and cultural differences among national groups. Reformers and local officials tended to see the largest immigrant groups as the most troublesome and neglected to recognize the importance of public socializing in exposing the poor to police discipline. Buenos Aires, like most cities of the United States, changed from a raucous, congested urban place to a well-ordered city as the rate of foreign immigration crested and the expansion of the built environment improved residents' opportunities for privacy. Overall, disorder declined as the city modernized, but violent crime held steady and poverty crime increased. An unprofessional and underpaid police department was increasingly less effective in meeting the challenges of growing urban crime. In Buenos Aires as well as in the United States, the middle and upper classes claimed a disproportionate share of police power for the protection of their residential and commercial properties. The obligation to enforce health and welfare codes and protect federal officials and federal buildings during an era of violent political confrontations further diluted the effectiveness of the police force of the Argentine capital.

The reality of rising crime rates in Buenos Aires does not relate directly to the ineffectiveness of the police. Property crimes declined in the United States during these same years, despite a slight decrease in the ability of the police to apprehend offenders. Property crime, as illustrated in Buenos Aires, correlated in the short term with the interaction between opportunity and economic conditions. When poverty was widespread and open displays of material goods were abundant, property crime increased.

While Buenos Aires shared the experience of increased civility or order with its industrializing counterparts in North America, the continuous rise in both property and personal crimes in the Argentine capital contrasts strongly with the urban United States. Historians of crime have maintained that a *U*-curve in criminality has characterized most Western cities.[31] The *U*-curve describes a pattern of decline in both property and violent crime from the midnineteenth century to the midtwentieth century followed by a period of increasing crime. Although its cultural forms and its modernization have clearly followed Western patterns, crime trends in Buenos Aires contradicted the *U*-curve. The exception of Buenos Aires cannot be explained fully, but the relationship of the city to the nation may provide an important key. Unlike Western nations, Argentina did not become an urban country between the 1880s and World War I. Argentine workers had few choices when migrating in search of a better life. An Argentine worker had some choices among provincial towns and the capital, but the choices were far more limited than those of French, British, or North American workers. While Buenos Aires expanded and presented the appearance of a modern city, the city lacked the broad industrial base of its North American counterparts. Argentina as a whole did not offer the fully developed industrial economy that supported the upward mobility and increasingly stable employment of the urban working classes in the United States. While North American immigrants adapted to urban life, immigrants in Buenos Aires were much more likely to be transient city-dwellers who would eventually seek rural employment in the rich agricultural hinterlands. Increasingly attracted to the city and trapped by circumstances unlike those of the highly mobile workers of the United States, unsuccessful residents of Buenos Aires may have increasingly vented their frustrations on the property and people around them. The decline of policing suggests that although Buenos Aires expanded commercially, the city failed to deliver the types of urban services, such as welfare and recreational facilities, that relieved the desperation and frustrations of the underclasses in many cities of the industrialized West.

Notes

1. This essay relies heavily on two articles by the author and Lyman L. Johnson: "Changing Criminal Patterns in Buenos Aires, 1890 to 1914," *Journal of Latin American Studies* (Nov. 1982): 359–80; *"Estadística criminal y acción policial en Buenos Aires, 1887–1914." Desarrollo Económico* (Apr.-June 1984): 109–22. Important analyses of criminal patterns and police behaviors in Western cities are Ted Robert Gurr, Peter N. Grabosky, and Richard C. Hula, *The Politics of Crime and Conflict: A Comparative History of Four Cities* (Beverly Hills, 1977); Eric Monkkonen, *Police in Urban America, 1860–1920* (Cambridge, 1981); Louise S. Shelley, *Crime and Modernization: The Impact of Industrialization and Urbanization on Crime* (Carbondale, 1981). Useful summaries of the literature are Ted Robert Gurr, "On the History of Violent Crime in Europe and America," in Hugh Davis Graham and Ted Robert Gurr, eds., *Violence in America: Historical and Comparative Perspectives* (Beverly Hills, 1979); Roger Lane, "Urban Police and Violence in Nineteenth Century America," in Norval Morris and Michael Tonry, *Crime and Justice: An Annual Review of Research*, vol. 2 (Chicago, 1980), pp. 1–43; Roger Lane, *Roots of Violence in Black Philadelphia, 1860–1900* (Cambridge, Mass. 1986), pp. 1–5.

2. Gino Germani, "The City as an Integrating Mechanism," in Glenn H. Beyere, ed., *The Urban Explosion in Latin America*, (Ithaca, 1967); David R. Goldfield and Blaine A. Brownell, *Urban America: From Downtown to No Town* (Boston, 1979); Zane L. Miller, *The Urbanization of Modern America: A Brief History* (New York, 1973); James R. Scobie, *Buenos Aires, Plaza to Suburb, 1870–1910* (New York, 1974); Charles S. Sargent, *The Spatial Evolution of Greater Buenos Aires, Argentina, 1870–1930* (Tempe, 1974).

3. Monkkonen, *Police*, pp. 65–85, 129–37, 148–55.

4. Lane, *Roots of Violence in Black Philadelphia*, pp 2–3.

5. Monkkonen, *Police*, pp. 65–85; Concepts of disorder and patterns of crime in London, Stockholm, Sydney and Calcutta are examined in Gurr et al., *The Politics of Crime and Conflict*, pp. 3–24.

6. Goldfield and Brownell, *Urban America*, pp. 243–63; Gino Germani, "Mass Immigration and Modernization in Argentina," in Irving Louis Horowitz, ed., *Masses in Latin America* (New York, 1970), pp. 289–330.

7. Lane, *The Roots of Violence in Black Philadelphia*, pp. 1–5, 144–61.

8. David Rock, *Politics in Argentina, 1890–1930: The Rise and Fall of Radicalism* (London: 1975); Roger Lane, *Policing the City: Boston, 1822–1885* (Cambridge, Mass., 1967); James F. Richardson, *The New York Police: Colonial Times to 1901* (New York, 1970).

9. Unless otherwise noted, all statistics on arrests and crimes reported in Buenos Aires have been drawn from *Anuario Estadístico de la Ciudad de Buenos Aires* for the years 1883 through 1914. The yearbooks reported

arrests by age, sex, ethnicity, and category of violation. This essay examines the arrests of males only. Each year, males accounted for at least 95 percent of people arrested for all crimes except prostitution. Female crime constituted a significantly different pattern of arrests than male crime and warrants a separate study. The Boston and New Haven statistics were analyzed by Eric Monkkonen, *Historical Methods* (Spring 1979), 63.

10. José Pantettieri, *Los trabajadores en tiempos de la inmigración masiva en Argentina, 1870–1910* (La Plata, 1966), pp. 43–48; Scobie, *Buenos Aires*, pp. 129–35.

11. Scobie, *Buenos Aires*, pp. 129–35.

12. Roberto Levillier, "Crime," in *General Census of the Population, Buildings, Trades and Industries of the City of Buenos Aires* (Buenos Aires, 1910), pp. 415.

13. For more detailed analyses of order arrests, see Blackwelder and Johnson, "Changing Criminal Patterns in Argentina," 363–74 and "Estadística criminal y acción policial," 109–18.

14. Roger Lane, *Violent Death in the City: Suicide, Accident, and Murder in Nineteenth-Century Philadelphia* (Cambridge, Mass., 1979), p. 10.

15. In the United States, the overall homicide rate rose from 1.2 deaths per 100,000 persons in 1900 to 8.4 by 1930. U.S. Bureau of the Census, *Historical Statistics of the United States, Colonial Times to 1970*, Bicentennial Edition, Part 1, (Washington, D.C., 1975), p. 414.

16. Lane, *Violent Death in the City*, pp. 54–141; Lane, *Roots of Violence in Black Philadelphia*, p. 2; Monkkonen, *Police*, pp. 74–77.

17. In North American cities, economic dislocations were also associated with a rise in property crime, but not with an increase in homicides. For a discussion of the U.S. pattern see Lane, *The Roots of Violence*, p. 2; Monkkonen, *Police*, pp. 77–85.

18. *Noberto Pinero Problemas de criminalidad* (Buenos Aires, 1888); Eusabio Gómez, *El problema penal argentino* (Buenos Aires, 1912); Lancelotti, M. A. *La criminalidad en Buenos Aires* (Buenos Aires, 1912).

19. Levillier, "Crime," p. 406.

20. Levillier, "Crime," pp. 395–98, 404–405. Carl Solberg discussed criminologists' references in the 1909 census and their attitudes toward immigrants in *Immigration and Nationalism; Argentina and Chile, 1980–1914*, (Austin, 1970), pp. 93–98.

21. Lawrence M. Friedman and Robert V. Percival, *The Roots of Justice: Crime and Punishment in Alameda County, California, 1870–1900* (Chapel Hill, N.C., 1981), pp. 106–107.

22. Lancelotti, *La Criminalidad*, pp. 41–45. In 1964, José León Pagano revived the nativist argument that immigrants were more likely to commit crimes than were native-born Argentines; *Criminalidad argentina* (Bue-

nos Aires, 1964), pp. 104–13; Blackwelder and Johnson, "Changing Criminal Patterns," 367.

23. Donna Guy has suggested that "Uruguayans" may have been predominantly European-born people who had been denied entrance to Argentina and settled in Uruguay, where immigration standards were less strict.

24. Levillier, "Crime," p. 415.

25. Eric Monkkonen, "Municipal Reports as an Indicator Source: The Nineteenth-Century Police," *Historical Methods* (Spring 1979), 57–65.

26. Samuel Walker discusses late-nineteenth century and twentieth century reforms in *A Critical History of Police Reform: The Emergence of Professionalism* (Lexington, Mass., 1977); Eric Monkkonen discusses the demand for policing in nineteenth century U.S. cities in *Police*; books that discuss the organization and reform of policing in specific cities are: Roger Lane, *Policing the City: Boston, 1822–1885* (Cambridge, Mass., 1967); Richardson, *The New York Police*; Wilbur R. Miller, *Cops and Bobbies: Police Authority in New York and London, 1830–1870* (Chicago, 1976).

27. Monkkonen, "Municipal Reports," 43.

28. Samuel Walker, *Popular Justice: A History of American Criminal Justice* (New York: 1980), pp. 13–144.

29. Belisario Roldán, a member of the Chamber of Deputies, claimed that farmer-soldiers were highly represented in the capital city's policy force just after the turn of the century. The composition of the police force and the role of the police in suppressing political unrest in the first decade of the twentieth century are discussed by Richard J. Walter in *The Socialist Party of Argentina, 1890–1930* (Austin, 1977), pp. 46–52, 79.

30. Blackwelder and Johnson, "Criminalidad y acción policial."

31. Lane, *Roots of Violence in Black Philadelphia*, pp. 2–6.

5

Prostitution and Female Criminality in Buenos Aires, 1875–1937

Donna J. Guy

The existence of female prostitution was viewed in two distinctive ways in the nineteenth century. European criminologists advanced the notion that prostitutes were born to commit crimes of sexual commerce. This theory, advocated by Pauline Tarnowsky, Caesar Lombroso, and William Ferrero, claimed that prostitutes had distinctive physical characteristics, particularly skull dimensions, that proved genetic inferiority. The women's condition was the same that afflicted male criminals who committed violent sociopathic acts. Phrenology was eventually rejected as a scientific discipline because of its racist and class-based assumptions. Nevertheless, social scientists in the early twentieth century in Latin America as well as in Europe continued to express the belief that prostitutes were biologically defective, and hence inherently criminal.[1]

At the same time that criminologists linked heredity to female prostitution, moral reformers advanced other theories. They explained female sexual commerce in an entirely different way, because they were convinced that evil men lured women into prostitution. Therefore, women were neither criminal nor defective; they were victims.

Moral reformers were concerned about a particular form of prostitution. White slavery, or the international traffic in women and children for purposes of sexual exploitation, was believed to be responsible for the presence of European women in bordellos throughout Latin America, the United States, Egypt, South Africa, and even in Europe. From the point of view of moral reformers, whenever foreign white women were found in legal bordellos abroad, the women were the victims. The governments that made bordellos legal businesses, and the men who lured women into overseas bordellos or cabarets, were the criminals.

These conflicting views of prostitution and criminality directly

affected the way Argentines and Europeans analyzed the consequences of legalized prostitution in Buenos Aires, the Argentine
capital and main port city. Female prostitution there was linked
both to lurid stories of white slavery and reports of bold and inherently criminal women. Both views represented a mixture of fact
and fantasy.

White Slavery in Buenos Aires

At the 1899 anti–white slavery congress sponsored by the National
Vigilance Association of Great Britain, a letter to the *Arbeiter Zeitung*
of Germany was read to the audience. It proclaimed that:

There are hundreds of wretched parents in Europe who do not know
whether their daughters are alive or dead, for they have suddenly van-
ished. . . . Well, we can tell where they have been brought to and what
has become of them. They are in Buenos Ayres. . . . This trade is a very
lucrative one, for the men in South America are of a very amorous disposition and "fair merchandise" from European lands easily finds buyers.
If anybody wants to find out how the girls are treated they may simply
take a walk along the Calle Juan and the Calle Lavalle, those two streets
that have been nicknamed by the people "Calle Sangre y Lagrima" (the
streets of tears and blood).[2]

At that same conference, reformers identified two branches of the
white-slave trade: one went through Constantinople, and the other
had Buenos Aires as its destination.

Many of the incidents that created this legend were often untrue
or exaggerated. Nevertheless, two facts were incontrovertible and
considered sufficient evidence to prove that local laws encouraged
white slavery. First of all, no one could deny that between 1875
and 1934 the Buenos Aires municipal council authorized prostitute registration and licensed bordellos. Second, most inscribed
women were foreign-born. As long as there as significant immigration of European females and legalized prostitution (see Table
1), Buenos Aires maintained its dubious reputation as the "Sin City"
of South America.[3]

Table 1
Nationality of Women Inscribed in Prostitutes' Registry, 1889–1901
According to Statistics Presented to the League of Nations, 1924

Years	Argentine	%	European	%	Latin American	%	Other	%	Total No.
1889	390	20	1,435	73	113	6	19	1	1,957
1890	135	16	687	79	37	4	8	1	867
1891	112	26	288	67	27	6	0	1	427
1892	108	30	222	61	32	9	1	1	363
1893	120	33	215	58	32	8	1	1	368
1894	86	33	146	56	27	10	1	1	260
1895	97	28	220	64	29	8	—	—	346
1896	89	27	208	64	29	7	3	2	329
1897	72	27	161	61	30	11	2	1	265
1898	79	32	192	66	21	7	—	5	292
1899	93	33	154	54	38	13	0	—	285
1900	81	24	219	65	38	10	1	1	338
1901	99	31	190	60	27	9	0	—	316

Argentine Theories of Criminality

The reality of legalized prostitution in Buenos Aires, however, was quite different from that imagined by European reformers. Whereas moral reformers argued that prostitute registration was a crime, local city authorities disagreed. In Buenos Aires, women were arrested if they refused to register or failed to identify their lodgings as a bordello. Furthermore, the *porteño* (Buenos Aires) system was based upon notions that conflicted with prevailing European theory.

Argentine politicians since the 1850s had invited European immigrants to settle in Argentina, a country with a small population that had been embroiled in civil wars since independence. Framers of the Argentine Constitution of 1853 hoped that immigrants would bring new skills and a civilizing influence. Argentine social scientists were therefore loathe to blame prostitution solely on hereditary factors. Instead, they hoped to analyze female prostitution as a curable social ill.

For this reason, Argentine social scientists did not necessarily view legalized prostitution as a source of criminality, but as the consequence of an influx of European women, the city's desire to create new sources of revenue, and the pernicious effect of socio-economic conditions on lower-class families. José Ingenieros, Argentina's leading positivist criminologist in the early twentieth century, believed that prostitution was labeled a crime only because men of certain classes found it convenient to criminalize the exchange of cash for sex by poor women. Ingenieros argued that women had the right to earn money through noncoercive sexual work. Dr. Eusebio Gómez, a popularizer of Lombroso's theories, admitted that Argentine data confirmed strong links between poverty and immorality.[4]

Because the causes of prostitution were viewed as a complex issue in Argentina, the monitoring of prostitution and bordello registration were haphazard at best. The image of an efficient but evil city government carefully controlling commercial sex through licensed bordellos was quite erroneous.

Argentine politicians tended to argue that prostitute registration was necessary to control venereal disease, rather than prevent criminality. Medical supervision of prostitution began in France in the early nineteenth century. The Argentine system was less coercive than the French one, which used a special squad of morals police to identify clandestine prostitutes. Rather than view legalized prostitution in Buenos Aires as an imitation of a European phenomenon, municipal regulation of prostitution and the subsequent police harrassment of clandestines in Buenos Aires can be better explained as local responses to urban social problems.

Police and Social Control in Buenos Aires

According to a recent study, in the first half of the nineteenth century, *porteño* urban problems had been resolved mostly by unauthorized police activities, often instigated by neighbors. Between 1832 and 1852, when Juan Manuel de Rosas was provincial governor and nominal head of the nation, "public and official attitudes in Buenos Aires about disorder and criminality took on an urgency in the absence of codified legal norms and continued arbitrary practices." Under these circumstances, police officials competed with judicial and municipal authorities for the right to control social unrest, and all resorted to unauthorized methods.[5]

The history of prostitution in Buenos Aires follows this pattern. City officials after the Rosas era continued to struggle against each other for the right to monitor unacceptable behavior. Over the years, these competing forces devised new ways to deal with prostitutes and disorderly women. What united their different methods was their refusal to confront the problem of female poverty, family coercion, and the lack of remunerative employment that caused women to contemplate prostitution. Instead, public officials tinkered with the nature and theory of control.

Throughout the nineteenth century, regardless of the legal status of prostitution, women accused of selling sexual favors came under the vigilance of municipal law. In the early years, poor urban women, regardless of evidence, were either ignored or rounded up and sent to military outposts for alleged sex trafficking. In 1832, for example, city police simply seized three hundred women "of doubtful character" and deported them to the southern frontier of Buenos Aires province "without any notice or investigation of their offences." They were most likely sent there to entertain the military.[6]

The fear of uncontrollable and unemployed women continued to haunt urban officials. After Rosas was overthrown in 1852, dancing halls called *academias de baile* or *peringundines*, often served as clandestine bordellos where fighting and scandalous behavior were frequent forms of diversion. These "sites of lower-class damnation" led police to close down such establishments at the request of neighbors.[7]

The absence of relevant laws in the 1850s and 1860s did not deter law-enforcement officers. Rather than focus on the prostitutes, however, they arrested customers who got into fights and created disturbances in the bordellos. In 1867, the chief of police ordered an "incessant prosecution" of all disruptable individuals who frequented pool halls, boarding houses, and "houses of immorality" by arresting such people for vagrancy. In order to identify such unsavory habitats, police created a list of hotels, boarding houses, dancing establishments, and bordellos in each district. According to its 1873 annual report, the Buenos Aires police continued to claim jurisdictional control over bordellos.[8]

Municipally Regulated Prostitution

In 1875, the Buenos Aires municipal council passed an ordinance designed to force police to focus on prostitutes, rather than their customers. Henceforth, poor women were defined as criminals if unemployment resulted in attempts to earn money through commercial sex without submitting to municipal and medical examination.

Prostitutes in Buenos Aires were turned into semicriminals if they admitted their profession and potential criminals if they did not. They could live alone or move into bordellos, but all were supposed to register and have weekly medical examinations in order to keep working. Once inside the bordello, women were treated like part-time jail inmates. Madames (*regentas*) could not leave the premises for more than twenty-four hours, and prostitutes had to return within two hours of sunset. Houses could display no signs. Prostitutes could not appear at windows or doors and could not provoke customers. When outside, all had to carry identity cards indicating their occupation and place of work. If a woman wanted to leave a life of prostitution, she was forced to provide good intentions by "volunteering" her services at a charitable institution for one month. Any woman who did not register and was discovered by neighbors or the police to be selling sexual favors would automatically be treated as a criminal and imprisoned for eight days.[9]

In response, the police resented the intrusion of the city council into what it considered a police matter. Once the ordinance became law, the chief of police informed his subordinates that any unlicensed madame would have her business shut down instead of being fined. Even though this directly violated the ordinance, the mayor (*intendente*) and municipal council failed to censure arbitrary police actions. Unfettered, the police closed down not just known brothels, but also any business run by males or females suspected by neighbors or the police of harboring clandestine prostitutes.

Indignant neighbors aided the police in their attempts to round up undesireable residents. Neighbors cared little whether taxes had been paid. Instead, they were concerned about the embarrassment of living in the same neighborhood where immoral women worked. Accusations from nearby dwellers were often sufficient to close down a business or force a woman out of her lodgings. According to the mayor's report of 1876, "Frequently the requests of respectable neighbors to close such establishments are passed on to the police; and the chief of police assures me that his department proceeds according to the wishes of the petitioner."[10]

In a short time, the municipality developed an approach to unlicensed, or clandestine, prostitution that used official sanctions and ad hoc police tactics. To the surprise of officials, the end results were disastrous and only led to more unlicensed establishments. Most of the difficulty stemmed from the council's decision to levy an extremely high license fee on bordellos because of a pressing need to raise money. The idea first came up in October 1874, when a council member suggested that "restaurants, cafés, and casinos frequented or operated by licencious women (*mujeres de vida licenciosa*)" pay a license fee of 10,000 pesos.[11]

That proposal became a reality the following year, when the city council ordered the registration of all tenement houses. For purposes of taxation, houses of prostitution were classified as first-class operations, regardless of size or location. In contrast hotels, rented houses, inns, and taverns included in this classification had to be in areas serviced by gaslights and contain at least ten rooms for rent. The 10,000 peso fee was more than that paid by most commercial establishments and banks.[12]

In 1878, the tax on first-class lodgings was raised to 15,000 pesos. Shortly thereafter, even city council members had second thoughts about the increase. At the 7 July 1880 meeting of the administrative board, the bordello tax was suspended "because this has caused an invasion of clandestine prostitution that has caused so much harm." Supporters of the board decision observed that "the more taxes are raised, the greater the effort to evade them," and the uniform bordello tax was unjust because "some houses can satisfy it and others not. The ones that cannot close down . . . only to reopen as casinos and clandestine bordellos."[13]

The tax was suspended, but only for a short time. The financial readjustment necessitated by the national economic collapse of 1890 led to a new formula of licensing and inspecting businesses in which bordellos paid higher fees than hotels. As late as 1902, 143 bordellos brought in 21 percent of commercial and industrial license fees although they represented less than 2 percent of the businesses.[14]

In contrast to the police or irate neighbors, the municipality's main concern was generating revenues, not eliminating prostitution. Despite many complaints of streetwalking and scandalous behavior by not too clandestine prostitutes, public officials were much more concerned with groups working out of bars, casinos, or unlicensed bordellos. These businesswomen more likely had the capital to pay the city bordello fee than the streetwalkers.

Although the licensing and fees received from bordellos might have enriched the coffers of the city treasury, the exorbitant fees and unlicensed bordellos presented problems for those attempting to hide sexual commerce and protect the city from venereal disease. Furthermore, legal bordellos guaranteed the visibility of prostitution. The need to keep track of bordellos made it easier to count establishments and analyze inmates on the basis of nationality. The existence of these facts overemphasized the immigrant component of prostitution and helped create Buenos Aires's internationally scandalous reputation as a center of the white-slave trade.

The Revolution of 1880 and Prostitution Reform Laws

The national revolt of 1880 that culminated in the naming of Buenos Aires as the permanent capital did little to change the arbitrary behavior of police and the municipal council. The revolution led to the appointment of Torcuato de Alvear as mayor, and he served until 1887. Although well known for his activities in beautifying the city, his accomplishments in the field of regulating prostitution have been ignored.[15]

Under his guidance, in less than a month the municipal council authorized the establishment of two municipally operated medical clinics for prostitutes and banned all prostitutes from the entire downtown area. If women tried to work in these areas, they were to be thrown into prison.[16] This reform, however, failed to keep prostitutes out of the young capital. Athough the need for medical dispensaries had been recognized by council members for years as a method of combatting venereal disease, their construction was delayed. Nevertheless, the plan to beautify the city went hand-in-hand with the idea of hiding or pushing away the marginal population.

The police resented the new laws, but they continued to arrest suspicious businesswomen as before. They closed business establishments and evicted almost anyone accused of clandestine prostitution. While municipal officials authorized similar punishments for reasons of hygiene, council members became offended by the uncontrolled activities of the police, particularly the imprisonment of prostitutes. Consequently, on 1 June 1881 physicians on the municipal-council hygiene committee told the chief of police to limit his forces' activities to preventing the opening of new houses and keeping prostitutes away from bordello windows and doors.[17]

Neither police activities nor the complaints about clandestine prostitution ceased. Instead, once the 15,000-peso fee was reinstituted, the problem became even worse. A September 1885 raid in San Nicolás parish resulted in the arrest of twenty-five madames and eighty-four prostitutes. Most of them lived in the three-hundred block of Tucumán Street, and the rest on Suipacha and Esmeralda. This mass arrest, instigated by neighbors, led to a legal rebellion by some of the arrested. On 4 December, fifteen madames complained to Intendente Alvear that they had been evicted for operating nonlicensed bordellos although the 1875 law mandated only fines. All the women signed the petition, indicating literacy, and most had Eastern European surnames. In response, council members admitted that, indeed, the women had not been treated correctly, and ordered that they all pay fines. Thereafter, any bordello still unlicensed would be closed. It was a pyrrhic victory for the outspoken regentas who, along with their employees, emerged vindicated but poorer.[18]

Summary arrests and closure of businesses continued as usual. In July 1886, Cándida Buschini, an Italian who operated a cigarette store on 25 de Mayo Street, complained of being closed down by the police for clandestine prostitution. Even though she accompanied her petition by signatures of neighbors who attested to her good character, the police inspector responded by stating unequivocally that clandestine prostitution was practiced there and thus the business had to be shut down.[19]

The only time such arbitrary procedures were not followed occurred when the police were at odds with the city. In October 1886, the municipality ordered the eviction of residents at Talcahuano Street 201, 203, 211, 225, and 227 for having practiced illegal prostitution. The police inspector cynically informed Mayor Alvear that such an action could only be carried out after it was determined that the residences were too unsanitary to be transformed into licensed bordellos. Therefore the police would not act.[20] Prostitutes were clearly caught in a power struggle between the police, the physicians, and the municipal government.

By the time Alvear left office, the lines of battle had been drawn in the war against vice in the city. The next mayor, Antonio V. Crespo, tried other tactics. Rather than close down clandestine bordellos, his administration tried to keep them operating as legal businesses. From archival documentation it appears that the arrest of clandestine prostitutes led to fines, rather than eviction, or orders to desist in business. Furthermore, under his guidance and that of his successor, the municipal council sanctioned the opening in 1888 of a Prostitutes' Registry (Dispensario de Salubridad), and the Prostitutes' Venereal Disease hospital (Sifilicomio) in 1889.[21]

Not only did Buenos Aires continue to condone bordellos and legalized prostitution, it refused to accept culpability for the existence of white slavery. In a legal judgment released in 1892, the city attorney defended the mayor's view that "The municipality cannot prevent the importation of deceived women from Europe who end up in houses of prostitution because its authority does not extend beyond the national capital."[22]

The municipality also had little control over prostitutes in Buenos Aires. After the initial success brought about by the opening of the Prostitutes' Registry (see Table 2), the number of women who registered for the first time declined dramatically until 1900 and only began to increase significantly in 1904.[23]

At the same time that the number of newly registered prostitutes continued to decline, the number of clandestine prostitutes rose. The only estimates available came from physicians. In 1880, for example, Dr. Emilio Coni claimed that there were 3,000 clandestines. By 1903, Dr. Enrique Revilla believed the number of clandestines to have risen to somewhere between 8,000 and 10,000. Calculations of illegal activity increased to 18,500 by 1915, a year when 510 women registered in bordellos for the first time, while 1,045 either changed residences or left the business altogether. The estimates of clandestinity can be accounted for partly by the haphazard enforcement of legalized prostitution, but mostly by the reality that women had to do something to put bread on the table for themselves and their families.[24]

Prostitution and Urban Crime in Buenos Aires

Although the increase in the number of clandestine prostitutes worried public officials, the criminal activities of men concerned them even more. As in many other cities, men, rather than women,

Table 2
Number of Prostitutes Registered For the First Time, 1889–1914

Year	Number	Year	Number
1889	2,007	1902	307
1890	871	1903	322
1891	427	1904	621
1892	367	1905	605
1893	368	1906	790
1894	261	1907	672
1895	344	1909	800
1896	320	1910	1,128
1897	249	1911	1,124
1898	295	1912	1,414
1899	274	1913	1,306
1900	339	1914	995
1901	317		

were the main perpetrators of major crimes. Misdemeanor offences, which included disorderly or scandalous behavior, were also principally male crimes at this time. In the early 1880s, for example, women constituted from 9 to 11 percent of the people arrested for disorderly behavior. In 1893, when legal bordellos were being closed down, only 3 percent of those arrested were women, and of those, only 32, or 26 percent, were identified as prostitutes. In terms of all misdemeanor crimes including drunkenness, in 1881–83, respectively, women comprised 11, 17, and 18 percent of the total, whereas in 1893 they formed only 4 percent. Clearly, although the police and the city council became adversaries on the issue of enforcing prostitution laws, the clandestines they arrested were but a minority of urban dwellers who came under police scrutiny.[25]

Not only were women far more law-abiding than men, the places where women were supposedly inciting men to violence were not the scenes of most crimes. Between 1887 and 1912, most crimes took place in the streets, private homes, or commercial businesses (see Table 3), not in cafés, bordellos, tenement houses, or bars.[26]

Reading the police *Memorias* in which these statistics were published, it is difficult to account for the intense scrutiny and concern for prostitution. In 1881, for example, surveys of different city

Table 3
Offences Classified According to Where They Took Place,
1887–1903, 1903–12

Place of Crime	1887–1903		1903–12	
	Total Number	%	Total Number	%
Public Way	30,143	32.24	37,065	40.07
Houses	28,641	30.63	35,554	38.44
Commercial Houses	15,786	16.88	10,871	11.75
Public Buildings	4,150	4.44	1,549	1.68
Buildings in Construction	1,083	1.16	1,365	1.48
Cafés, Hotels, etc.	4,128	4.41	3,587	3.88
Tenement Houses	5,205	5.57	1,578	1.71
Brothels	1,268	1.35	577	.62
Not Specified	1,229	1.32	345	.37

districts were published in an effort to justify staff increases. The report for Section 5, which included the Parque de Artillería, noted that the population of 14,700 resided mostly in tenement houses and that the area was dotted with sixty-three cafés, twenty-nine houses of prostitution, and a variety of inns and lodging houses. Such conditions produced all sorts of outrageous behavior, and according to the police, liquor and women were believed to incite the troubles. Women lured men into cafés and illegal gambling and dancing halls, most of which had access to bedrooms. These businesses were such an attraction that on the weekends, the district's population swelled to more than 19,000, yet only 20 police officers were on duty. That same year, other areas in the city, such as Section 20, which included La Boca, also cited the presence of commercial sex as a fundamental cause of sociopathic behavior.[27]

Four years later, the police continued to fear dangerous women, but still did not arrest them. The 1884–85 report included a letter from a policeman in charge of Section 3 who had arrested a mother for selling her daughter's sexual services to a bordello. She was caught while patiently waiting outside with another daughter. To the policeman's dismay, the judge dismissed the case. The case of the immoral mother was just the tip of the iceberg as far as he was concerned, since in his district there were more than one hundred clandestine bordellos employing more than 500 women. He accused these women of luring young girls in the streets and then raffling them off to the highest bidder. He may have complained and accused, but only occasionally arrested, because in the entire city that year only 364 women were arrested for disorderly behavior.[28]

The letter is unusual because individual cases were rarely printed in annual police reports, and because it accused a woman of pimping her own child, rather than the typical complaint of husbands, fathers, or nonrelated males as procurers. It also portrayed the women accused of clandestine prostitution as independent of males, devoid of principles, and threats to the community. These were the women who corrupted their children and lured men into trouble, infecting them with diseases and encouraging them to commit crimes. To the Buenos Aires police, such disorderly women were the antithesis of the white-slave victim, typically portrayed as an innocent woman victimized by evil men, often foreigners. Rather than having been coerced into a life of prostitution by men, these women victimized each other, and, in their quest for money, victimized men as well.

Not all policemen, however, were in agreement that women were the cause of urban crime. The year after the immoral mother sold her child to a bordello, two policemen published an exposé, *La prostitutción en Buenos Aires*. It began with an open letter to their chief, Marcos Paz, complaining of the impossibility of maintaining social order so long as housing shortages led to tenement houses wherein

disorder prevails in habitations shared by various families and individuals of both sexes and all ages, most of whom do not know how to restrain their baser instincts . . . It is logical that from these places are recruited victims, many of whom have been influenced by the immoral conditions there.[29]

These two officers also believed that public authorities were responsible for increased clandestine prostitution in Buenos Aires. Few legal bordellos operated because of municipal harrassment and overly stringent regulations. According to the national Commercial Code, young women could work in these establishments before they reached the age of majority. City officials did nothing to prevent pimps from financing houses that technically were operated by women, and a pimps' club with two hundred members operated openly from a restaurant and café. Under such circumstances, the municipality had no right to insist that police hector prostitutes.[30]

A contemporary and fellow officer, Adolfo Batiz, offered his own explanations of the causes of prostitution, both official and clandestine, in Buenos Aires in the 1880s. As did the others, he saw two distinct patterns, one associated with white slavery, part of which involved pimping by husbands and fathers, and another, also based upon family coercion, but rooted in Argentine socioeconomic conditions. Police had few hopes of rescuing prostitutes, because

> their own parents and relatives have forced them to sell their bodies, and they agree to do it because of their extreme poverty. Under these circumstances young girls who dedicate themselves to commercial sex believe that they are doing a good deed since the product of their dishonest work feeds the members of their families.[31]

The Anti–White Slavery Campaign in Buenos Aires

Just before the outbreak of World War I, international criticism of legalized prostitution in Buenos Aires led to the passage of a national law to deal with white slavery. The bill was sponsored by the country's first socialist deputy, Alfredo L. Palacios, and it mandated jail sentences for men who forced minors to engage in commercial sex. If the guilty party were a relative, husband, or tutor, he would lose rights to exercise parental authority, or *patria potestad*. Foreign-born pimps faced deportation if convicted of white slavery more than once. Only female bordello operators would not be accused of contributing to the sexual enslavement of a woman unless she knowingly took in minors (women under the age of twenty-two).[32]

In his accompanying speech, Palacios specifically mentioned how embarrassed he was that Buenos Aires was known in Europe as "the worst of all the centers of the immoral commerce in women."[33] He also emphasized that it was a matter of national shame that Argentina allowed the illegal traffic in young women to operate anywhere in the republic. In order to eliminate the scandal, female minors, even if they were prostitutes, had to have legal protection from pimps.

When the bill emerged from the Chamber of Deputies' legislative commission on which Palacios served, its modifications included legal protection of adult females. According to the revision, if adult women were forced into prostitution because their consent had been given through deception or the threat of violence, the accused would face from one to three years of prison. With this provision, the projected law for the first time ensured that any woman forced into prostitution involuntarily, whether by a stranger or a relative, could seek legal redress.[34]

When the Ley Palacios was enacted in 1913, the reaction of the European press was quite favorable despite the fact that the measure did nothing to restrict municipal bordellos. Even so, it appeared to have a salutary effect, because it forced many foreign pimps to leave the capital city. According to the National Vigilance Association, "The effect [of the bill was] electrical; according to the investigation department no less than 2,000 procurers . . . left the capital as if fleeing from an earthquake."[35]

The passage of the Ley Palacios, followed by the outbreak of World War I the next year, should have put an end to Buenos Aires's evil reputation. If all the foreign pimps had left town and few could return because the war interrupted the migratory flow from Europe to the New World, the white-slavery problem should have disappeared. The diminution of female immigration to Argentina, however, seemed to make little difference to those who were concerned about white slavery in Buenos Aires. Sensationalist tracts like *In the Grip of the White Slave Trader*, published in London during the war, warned English women that

One cannot escape . . . from one thought in connection with the traffic as regards English girls. On all sides it is admitted that the hotbed of this abominable trade is the Argentine.[36]

This anonymous publication then reported that a guide to the bordellos of the world, published in France, listed addresses of seventy expensive *porteño* bordellos where "The English girl commands the highest price, and it is to the Argentine that she is generally exported."

The outbreak of World War I, along with the subsequent enactment of new Argentine immigration laws in 1921, did more to halt the influx of European pimps and prostitutes than any well-intentioned efforts of boat inspectors or the Ley Palacios. Many traffickers who had left Argentina in the wake of the 1913 law became trapped in Europe. In general, few immigrants arrived in Buenos Aires between 1914 and 1918 (see Table 4), and Argentine women registered more frequently than in the prewar years.[37]

After the war, however, the proportion of foreign-born women in *porteño* houses began to increase, and Europeans again considered Argentina a hotbed of white slavery. Even though the number of women who registered at the Prostitutes' Registry never again equaled yearly entries before World War I (see Table 5), foreign-born women were still overrepresented among the few legal prostitutes.[38]

The Police and the Prostitute

There were clear indications from 1913 onward that national laws would not easily resolve the relationship between prostitution, white slavery, and views of female criminality in Argentina. The Ley Palacios was more a symbolic than real threat to potential pimps or traffickers. In fact, the law encouraged prostitute victimization by police, as well as by other immoral men and women. Unlike its stated goals, the Ley Palacios rarely protected women mistreated by husbands, relatives, or strangers. Instead, Buenos Aires police used it to justify harsher campaigns against women generally and unlicensed prostitutes specifically.

The Buenos Aires 1913 annual police report discussed the Ley Palacios under the heading of "Social Morality" (*Moralidad Social*). According to the police, the law had not been nearly as effective as its intent. Pimps were a difficult problem "because they undertake their activities in secret and evasive ways," that frustrate law enforcement. Consequently, there had only been sixteen cases— four involving parents, three spouses, and the rest by third parties.[39]

While police doubted the ability to pursue perfidious men, they seemed more positive about ensaring insidious women. They included a long report entitled "Traffic in Children" to advance this view. While one might presume that it recounted efforts to eliminate white slavers from the capital city following the passage of the Ley Palacios, instead it told a very different cautionary tale. Claiming that "in this capital there exists a real traffic in children,"

Table 4

Nationality of Newly Registered Women, 1910–23

Nationality	1910	1911	1912	1913	1914	1915	1916	1917	1918	1919	1920	1921	1922	1923
Argentine	14%	23%	21%	25%	16%	25%	27%	35%	39%	41%	15%	15%	25%	29%
Eastern European*	27	25	24	29	4	16	12	11	11	3	10	21	25	24
French	20	25	26	17	17	12	16	7	10	20	35	41	28	30
Italian	7	9	9	12	15	13	14	12	3	10	—	7	9	6
Spanish	8	8	12	10	18	24	22	23	26	19	15	4	5	6
Uruguayan	20	9	5	5	23	4	6	6	7	7	—	8	1	1
Others	4	—	3	2	7	6	3	6	4	—	25	4	7	4

*Includes Austro-Hungarian, Russian, Rumanian, Polish, and Ukranian.

Table 5
Newly Registered Women, Buenos Aires, 1913–34

Year	Number	Year	Number	Year	Number
1913	1,306	1921	143	1929	——
1914	995	1922	348	1930	34
1915	510	1923	335	1931	217
1916	406	1924	427	1932	193
1917	279	1925	669	1933	250
1918	195	1926	137	1934	249
1919	215	1927	——		
1920	20	1928	——		

police reported that midwives were selling young infants of unmarried women.

Proof of this trade could be obtained by opening to the classified section of any *porteño* newspaper, where a typical advertise-
ment read: "Midwife Canale takes in boarders, children are also
taken in" (*se hace cargo del niño*). While listing two pages of similar
announcements, the police claimed they had proof that these "were
evidently related to this type of traffic."[40]

Obviously this report had little to do with the white-slavery
aspects of the Ley Palacios. Instead, it dealt with another facet of
parental authority, the unwillingness of unmarried fathers and
mothers to assume responsibility for their illegitimate offspring.
Women who delivered the children often helped the couples by
finding adoptive parents. Rather than consider this form of female
work an appropriate solution to a pressing social problem, the police
considered it a violation of the law.[41]

Police attitudes toward midwives paralleled their vigilance of
female prostitutes. Unable to stop the men who often forced women
on the streets or into clandestine bordellos, the police responded
by creating a new category of disorderly conduct. Scandalous behavior (*escándalo*) had been a designation used by the province of Buenos Aires as early as 1889 and pertained to prostitutes attracting
clients, corrupting the morals of a minor, obscene acts and ges-
tures, or public nudity.[42]

By 1915, scandalous behavior in the national capital became the
female counterpart to disorderly behavior, and most of the women

arrested for this crime were prostitutes. Women constituted 1,960, or 80 percent, of those guity of scandal. Equally important, 66 percent of the women arrested were self-identified prostitutes, and 47 percent were Argentines. This meant that the law was being used principally to control unlicensed sexual commerce, and Argentine women were among those most frequently brought in. Meanwhile, traffickers and pimps were almost ignored, because in the same year only twenty-six cases of white slavery were investigated in Buenos Aires. As a result, 44 people were detained.[43]

Scandalous behavior remained a female crime in Buenos Aires as long as prostitution within authorized bordellos continued to define the difference between legal and clandestine prostitution. This is evident (see Table 6) in the arrest records for 1919 until 1927.[44]

Prostitutes, both native-born and foreign, were the principal targets of police arrests. Between 1920 and 1930, self-identified prostitutes comprised 50 to 79 percent of all women detained for scandalous behavior. The proportion of Argentine women ranged from 32 percent in 1922 to 73 percent in 1927. During these years, more than two thousand women were arrested annually for this misdemeanor offence, a figure that suggests that women were caught streetwalking as well as working in suspicious jobs.[45]

While all this was happening, Buenos Aires police officials professed dismay at their inability to arrest pimps and other male undesireables. Police simplistically blamed female sexual commerce on the immigrant population, several times advocated the passage of stricter anti-immigrant vagrancy and antipimping laws, and lamented that national legislators ignored their entreaties. In the meantime, arrests of pimps' victims, increasingly native-born, were the only way city police could demonstrate their efficiency. Unfortunately, few people paid attention to the adverse consequences of the Ley Palacios.[46]

Table 6
Arrests for Scandalous Behavior, By Sex, 1919–27

	1919	1920	1921	1922	1923	1924	1925	1926	1927
Males	394	581	327	432	683	724	1,129	1,092	617
%	17	29	12	15	25	26	28	25	16
Females	1,954	1,448	2,377	2,446	2,098	2,057	2,919	3,320	3,254
%	83	71	88	85	75	74	72	75	84

The Abolition of Legalized Prostitution

In 1928, a scandal erupted that threatened to embarrass city and national officials at the highest levels. Several members of the Buenos Aires police were put on trial for having falsified official documents. As a result, underaged women worked in the few legal bordellos. According to one German pimp, Herr Koster, "All that was necessary was a photograph, and, after that had been obtained, the certificate was issued with the space for fingerprints and signature in blank, to be filled in at a later date." The charges against the police were eventually dropped after Hipólito Yrigoyen was reelected president that year.[47]

After yet another prostitution-related scandal erupted in May 1930, *porteño* politicians decided it was finally time to separate the city from the prostitution business. In December 1930, José Guerrico, the Buenos Aires mayor, issued a decree abolishing municipally licensed prostitution in the national capital. In his prefatory remarks, the mayor admitted that Buenos Aires was considered a center of international white slavery. More important, he recognized the validity of critics who argued that legalized prostitution was an ineffective farce. To rectify the situation, he decreed that the city would no longer monitor bordellos and ordered the closing of the Prostitutes' Registry. Then he created a committee to organize an anti–venereal disease campaign.[48]

It was one thing to make a decree and quite another to have the order carried out. Between 1930 and 1934, mayors bickered with members of the municipal council until all came to recognize the inevitability of abolishing legalized prostitution. Finally, they agreed to ban bordellos after 31 December 1934 and replace prostitution ordinances with ones that offered medical care, repatriation, or help for those who left bordellos in finding "honest jobs." More comprehensive municipal anti–venereal disease campaigns were also authorized.[49]

In order to implement the new law, Mayor Vedia y Mitre ordered the burning of all books and papers at the Prostitutes' Registry that contained personal data. This included all the identity booklets prostitutes and maids were supposed to carry. Then, three days later, the municipality ordered that police arrest anyone who encouraged licentious behavior (*toda incitación al libertinaje o lo que signifique un atentado a la moralidad y buenas costumbres*). This placed the police at a disadvantage, because they could not officially identify women who, until recently, had been prostitutes. The ordinance also demonstrated that it remained unclear whether prostitution itself was illegal.[50]

In response to the new laws, during the first year of the ban, police created a new category of scandalous behavior, one that was appended by the word *incitar* (to incite). For that crime, 2,910 women were arrested, compared to 23 males, whereas 237 women were arrested for scandalous behavior that did not incite, compared to 1,017 males. The new category was clearly designed to keep women from luring men with sexual propositions. Of the 2,910 women arrested, 907 (31 percent) were self-identified prostitutes, and 1,197 (41 percent) were unemployed. In 1936, almost 5,000 women were brought in on similar charges, 51 percent of whom were prostitutes and only 12 percent of whom were unemployed. Police had defined the ordinances in such a way as to make prostitution, rather than bordello operations, an illegal activity.[51]

They justified their actions in 1935 by stating that they had been systematically excluded from controlling prostitution by the municipality's efforts to rehabilitate women, although it was their duty to protect the youth of the city. For that reason, they believed it was necessary to watch the women who were no longer required to have medical examinations.[52]

Even though the city of Buenos Aires banned licensed bordellos after 1934, it remained unclear whether prostitution itself was illegal and what effect provincial bordellos would have on the ban in the capital. Even after the Argentine Congress enacted the Law of Social Prophylaxis in December 1936, designed to end all municipally licensed bordellos as well as institute a national program of venereal-disease treatment, these questions remained in the minds of policemen, criminologists, and jurists.[53]

In 1938, Vicente M. Signorelli, a police officer, published an article in the *Revista de Policía y Criminalística* about the motivation of female prostitutes. There he cited many authors who supported nineteenth-century criminological views that prostitution was a female form of criminality that acted as "an escape valve" to keep women from committing more violent crimes.[54] Yet, when he analyzed the statistics of women arrested for inciting scandal, he noted that in 1935 and 1936, most of those arrested were either self-identified prostitutes or unemployed. Fearing an increase in the number of women who would label their work prostitution, Signorelli lauded the efforts of the police to arrest such women, but argued that vocational rehabilitation for unemployed women would be the best deterrent.[55]

Criminologist Enrique Aftalión was less sanguine about the prospects for controlling prostitution, because the Law of Social Prophylaxis was imprecise. Highly influenced by the international anti–white slavery campaign, the law's intent was to eliminate licensed bordellos. Consequently, it neither specified whether the act of prostitution itself was a crime nor whether a residence habitually used by a prostitute for commercial sex was a bordello. As a result, many women were being unjustly accused of violating Articles 15 and 17.[56]

Over the years, the number of violations were few and far between. In 1939, there were only 344 cases, and by 1945, they had dwindled to 70. While some saw this decrease as a sign of improved morality and police efficiency, the veracity of this view must be challenged. The fact that thousands of women were being arrested in Buenos Aires each year for inciting scandalous behavior, a crime that could be prosecuted, while few men or women were convicted of violating the national law, suggested that the implementation of the Law of Social Prophylaxis resulted in police harrassment of suspected prostitutes in the same way that the Ley Palacios had years earlier.[57]

Dr. Felicitas Klimpel, a noted criminologist and feminist, studied the statistics of women jailed in Buenos Aires for nonmisdemeanor offences between 1936 and 1942. She discovered that in those years, no more than 16 percent of these women had been convicted of violating the Law of Social Prophylaxis. This led her to conclude that "Prostitution is neither a form of criminality nor a substitute for criminal behavior. It is a job, a profession, one that some women pursue because they are mentally unprepared for other forms of work."[58] Once again, these conclusions, particularly the claim of female mental instability, must be reexamined with misdemeanor arrests for inciting scandalous behavior in mind.

Obviously, the enactment of the Law of Social Prophylaxis did little to rid the city of prostitutes or end the sexual exploitation of women. Throughout the 1930s and 1940s, judges, police, and politicians all bickered over whether the prostitution clauses mandated that Argentina criminalize prostitution or merely end municipally licensed bordellos. In the long run, the Social Prophylaxis Law was most successful at improving Argentina's reputation among international reformers.

Throughout the era of municipally licensed bordellos, police, criminologists, and politicians all argued about the relationship of prostitution to criminality. European theories served to confuse, rather than clarify, the basic problems confronted in Buenos Aires because of their concerns about heredity and the nationality of women who registered in *porteño* bordellos. These issues were unrelated to the gender structure of the labor force, overcrowding in urban tenements, problems of familial coercion, and the government's inability to enforce reforms to limit the power of heads of family.

At the same time that theories muddled perceptions of urban reality, an analysis of prostitution control in the Argentine national capital reveals other disturbing features. Law enforcement related more to power struggles among the police, politicians, and public-health physicians than a true response to the social and medical dangers presumed to be associated with female prostitution. Laws designed to protect women were often used as justification of campaigns to harrass them. If men could not be prosecuted for the problem, police simply found ways to blame women.

Under these circumstances, it was inevitable that the prostitution problem would not disappear in Buenos Aires. Even if all Europeans forgot about the city's relationship to the white-slave trade, Argentines would continue to use the prostitution issue as a symbolic way to confront a variety of gender, class, and political issues. Until these issues could be examined in a more direct fashion, the city's prostitutes would continue to be harrassed by arbitrary and capricious methods, regardless of their legal rights.

Notes

The research for this article was conducted under the auspices of a National Endowment for the Humanites Senior Summer Research Fellowship, a Fulbright-Hayes Senior Lectureship, and a University of Arizona Sabbatical Fellowship.

1. Pauline Tarnowsky, *Étude Anthropométrique sur les Prostituées et les Voleuses* (Paris, 1869); Caesar Lombroso and William Ferrero, *The Female Offender* (London, 1895).

2. National Vigilance Association, *Congress of the White Slave Traffic* (London, 1899), p. 86.

3. Included in reply of Jacinte Fernández, judge of the Political Division, Buenos Aires Police, to League of Nations, 27 Aug. 1924, National Vigilance Association (NVA), Box 111, Fawcett Library, London Polytechnic (London).

4. Donna J. Guy, "White Slavery, Public Health, and the Socialist Position on Legalized Prostitution in Argentina, 1913–1936," *Latin American Research Review* 23:3 (1988), 60–80.

5. Mark D. Szuchman, "Disorder and Social Control in Buenos Aires, 1819–1860," *Journal of Interdisciplinary History* (Summer 1984): 108.

6. Richard W. Slatta, *Gauchos and the Vanishing Frontier* (Lincoln, 1983), p. 66.

7. María Sáenz Quesada, *El estado rebelde, Buenos Aires entre 1850/1860* (Buenos Aires, 1982), p. 246.

8. Argentine Republic, *Memoria de la policía de Buenos Aires* (hereinafter *Memorias*), 1876, p. 564; 1873, p. 484.

9. Buenos Aires Municipality, *Actas de la Comisión Municipal de la Ciudad de Buenos Aires* (hereinafter *Actas*), 5 Jan. 1875, pp. 317–23.

10. Buenos Aires Municipality, *Memoria*, 1876, pp. 104–105.

11. Buenos Aires Municipality, *Actas*, 15 Oct. 1874, p. 259.

12. Buenos Aires Municipality, *Actas*, 30 Oct. 1875, pp. 443–45. Only importers of iron goods and military hardware had to pay such fees. See 1870 tax chart that accompanied the complaint of Manuela Benites for having her tavern closed down because of charges of clandestine prostitution. Archivo Histórico de la Municipalidad de Buenos Aires (hereinafter AHMBA), Salud Pública, 1880, leg. 26.

13. Buenos Aires Municipality, *Actas*, 7 July 1880, pp. 66–67.

14. Buenos Aires Municipality, *Memoria*, 1903, p. 69.

15. James R. Scobie, *Buenos Aires, Plaza to Suburb, 1870–1910* (New York, 1974), pp. 109–13, recounts Alvear's efforts to beautify the city.

16. Dr. José Manuel Irizar, "Servicio sanitario de la prostitución," *Anales del Departamento Nacional de Higiene*, 1904, pp. 108–109.

17. Letter from the Sección Higiene of the Municipal Council to President of the Municipality, 1 June 1881. Signed by Drs. Emilio R. Coni, José María Ramos Mejía, and Domingo Parodi. AHMBA, Salud Pública, 1881, leg. 25.

18. The sequence of events began with a petition from neighbors on 30 June 1885. AHMBA, Salud Pública, 1885, leg. 42. Then the police con-

firmed what neighbors said in a letter to the Intendente, 11 Sept. 1895. After the women were arrested, they filed a complaint that included the data on the houses. Petition of 19 Sept. 1885.

19. Petition of Cándida Buschini, 22 July 1886, AHMBA, Salud Pública, 1886, leg. 99.

20. Letter of Police to Intendente, 2 Oct. 1886, AHMBA, Salud Pública, 1886, leg. 99. Note from the Municipal Attorney (Asesor) to the Intendente regarding his order to evict people from Talcahuano Street.

21. See the report of the arrest and fine levied on Ramona Risso for clandestine prostitution, 15 Oct. 1887, AHMBA, Salud Pública, 1886, pp. 263–66.

22. Municipality of Buenos Aires, *Dictámenes de la Asesoría Municipal, 1878–1894*, vol. 3 (Buenos Aires, 1896), pp. 208–10.

23. These figures are similar to, but do not agree exactly with, the statistics offered by Jacinte Fernández. Buenos Aires Municipality, *Anuario estadístico de la ciudad de Buenos Aires*, 1900, p. 225; 1905, p. 216; 1907, p. 210; 1909, p. 95; 1911, p. 185; 1913, p. 94; 1914, p. 100.

24. Dr. Emilio R. Coni, *Higiene pública. El servicio sanitario de la ciudad de Buenos Aires* (Buenos Aires, 1880), p. 12; Dr. Juan Lazarte, *Sociología de la prostitución* (Buenos Aires, 1945), pp. 132–33; Dr. Enrique Revilla, "El ejercicio de la prostitución en Buenos Aires, Proyecto de Ordenanza elevado a la Intendencia Municipal," *Archivos de Psiquiatría y Criminología y Ciencias Afines* (Enero 1903): 77; Buenos Aires City, *Anuario estadístico de la ciudad de Buenos Aires*, 1915–23, p. 133.

25. Buenos Aires Police, *Memoria*, 1881, pp. 260–61; 1882, pp. 262–63; 1883, pp. 118–19; 1883, pp. 63–65.

26. Buenos Aires Municipality, *Anuario estadístico de la ciudad de Buenos Aires*, 1903, p. 243; *Statistical Year-Book for the City of Buenos Aires*, 1912, p. 246.

27. Buenos Aires Police, *Memoria*, 1881, pp. 184–89, 230–31.

28. Buenos Aires Police, *Memoria*, 1884–85. Letter of Pedro A. Costa to Police Chief Enrique García Merou, 13 Sept. 1884, pp. 20–23; misdemeanor statistics, p. 252.

29. C. y A., *La prostitución en Buenos Aires* (Buenos Aires, 1885), p. iv.

30. C. y A., *La prostitución en Buenos Aires*, 2–12.

31. Adolfo Batiz, *Buenos Aires, la ribera y los prostíbulos en Buenos Aires* (Buenos Aires, n.d.), p. 89.

32. Argentine Republic, Cámara de Diputados, *Diario de Sesiones*, 8 Aug. 1913, pp. 838–39.

33. Argentine Republic, Cámara de Diputados, *Diario de Sesiones*, pp. 838–42.

34. Argentine Republic, Cámara de Diputados, *Diario de Sesiones*, 17 Sept. 1913, pp. 321–22.

35. *Vigilance Record*, No. 11 (Nov. 1913), p. 91.

36. *In the Grip of the White Slave Trader* [By the Author of *The White Slave Traffic*] (London, n.d.), pp. 76, 83–84.

37. "Nationality of Newly Registered Prostitutes in Buenos Aires for the Years 1910 to 1923, Inclusive," League of Nations, *Report of the Special Body of Experts on Traffic in Women and Children* 2:19; Victor Mirelman, "The Jews in Argentina (1890–1930): Assimilation and Particularism," Ph.D. Thesis, Columbia University (1973), p. 13.

38. 1913–19 statistics from the Dispensario de Salubridad. Buenos Aires Municipality, *Statistical Year-Book for the City of Buenos Aires*, 1913, p. 94; 1914, p. 100; *Anuario estadístico de la ciudad de Buenos Aires*, 1915–23, p. 133; "El problema de la prostitución," *Archivos de la Secretaría de Salud Pública* (Nov. 1948): 419.

39. Buenos Aires Police, *Memoria*, 1913, pp. 11–12.

40. Buenos Aires Police, *Memoria*, 1913, pp. 227–28.

41. Buenos Aires Police, *Memoria*, 1913, pp. 231–35.

42. Buenos Aires Province, *Reglamento general de policía de la Provincia de Buenos Aires* (La Plata, 1889), p. 128.

43. Buenos Aires Police, *Memoria*, 1915–16, pp. 28, 288–89.

44. Buenos Aires Police, *Memoria*, 1919–27, passim.

45. Francis Korn, *Buenos Aires: Los huéspedes del 20* (Buenos Aires, 1974), p. 142n.

46. Buenos Aires Police, *Memoria de la policía*, 1916, pp. 388–89; 1919–20, p. 38; 1923, pp. 43–46; 1924, pp. 9–10; 1926, pp. 9–10.

47. Extract from letter of Mrs. Lighton Robinson, 3 Dec. 1928, NVA, Box 111, Co1A.

48. Municipalidad de Buenos Aires, Decreto derogando la ordenanza sobre la reglamentación de la prostitución, 24 Dec. 1930, AGN, Ministerio del Interior, 1931 Expedientes, leg. 8, no. 6, 362-M.

49. See the debates in Buenos Aires Municipality, *Actas*, 15 Apr. 1932, pp. 681–82; 3 Oct. 1933, pp. 2184–86; 5 May 1933, pp. 758–59; 18 Sept. 1934, pp. 2137–38, 2150–52; 20 Nov. 1934, pp. 2897–2901; 7 Dec. 1934, p. 3368; 18 Dec. 1934, pp. 3712–14.

50. Ordinances and decrees reprinted in Buenos Aires Police, *Memoria*, 1934, pp. 242–45.

51. Buenos Aires Police, *Memoria*, 1935, p. L; 1936, p. L.

52. Buenos Aires Police, *Memoria*, 1935, p. 26.

53. The deputies' debates on this law can be found in Argentine Republic, Cámara de Diputados, *Diario de Sesiones*, 26 Sept. 1935, pp. 552–68; 9

Dec. 1936, pp. 939–49. The Senate debates are located in Argentine Republic, Senado, *Diario de Sesiones*, 18 Sept. 1936, pp. 261–84; 17 Dec. 1936, pp. 303–11.

54. Vicente M. Signorelli, "La mujer y la prostitución," *Revista de Policía y Criminalística* 11: No. 12–13 (1938): 52.

55. Signorelli, "La mujer y la prostitución," 53.

56. Dr. Enrique Aftalión, "Prostitución, proxenetismo y delito; Estudio crítico de la jurisprudencia sobre los artículos 15 y 17 de la Ley 12.331," *Revista de Policía y Criminalística* (April-June 1940): 4–5.

57. José León Pagano, (h), *Criminalidad argentina* (Buenos Aires, 1964), p. 136.

58. Dr. Felicitas Klimpel, *La mujer, el delito y la sociedad* (Buenos Aires, 1945), pp. 220–22.

6

Changing Arrest Patterns in Three Argentine Cities

Buenos Aires, Santa Fe, and Tucumán, 1900–30

Lyman L. Johnson

"The greatest of evils and the worst of crimes is poverty."
George Bernard Shaw, preface to *Major Barbara*.

The related topics of crime and policing are among the least-studied areas of Latin American social history. There is encouraging evidence offered in a series of recent publications that these topics are now beginning to attract the attention they deserve. The criminological literature devoted to Latin America provides many examples of methodological sophistication and conceptual ingenuity, but there has been no effort, as yet, to create a single theoretical and interpretive context from these analyses of individual cases separated in space and time.[1] As a result, the elemental characteristics of either criminal activity or police response for Latin America cannot be identified. Put another way, current understanding of crime and policing is largely derivative, an analogue of development studies before the advent of dependency theory. To redress these weaknesses, sources and methods that will promote the comparative analysis of these topics across political boundaries and over substantial periods of time must be identified.

Export-dominated capitalist development of Latin American affected both political culture and class relationships in the region. As a result, the political labels and social classifications derived from the historical experience of Western Europe and the United States are no longer uncritically applied to Latin America. Did the range and distribution of criminal activities and police responses also reflect in significant ways the influence of this form of economic development? To explore these questions further, criminological theory developed through the study of crime and policing in industrialized societies must be tested in the Latin American context.

The most developed and accessible area of scholarly inquiry on crime and the police is an effort to explain the relationship between changing criminal patterns and the combined effects of urbanization and industrialization, a process commonly referred to as modernization.[2] Scholarly interest in these relationships first appeared in the nineteenth century with the development of modern social science and was reinforced recently by interest in urban history. In general, investigators found that both the level and the character of crime—the mix of felony and misdemeanor offenses—changed as cities expanded in population and function. Because these issues lend themselves to quantitative analysis, the most influential studies on this topic have been located temporally in the statistical era, especially the period after 1880.[3]

This essay is an effort to examine police responses to a range of criminal and other antisocial acts in three Argentine cities during the period from 1900 to 1930. The primary sources for this comparative analysis are annual reports produced by municipal and provincial statistical departments. Although municipal reports are a commonly used source for the study of crime and policing in the United States and Europe, they have been generally ignored by Latin Americanists.[4] Nearly every capital city and many secondary cities in Latin America began publishing some form of annual statistical review by the end of the nineteenth century. Although coverage and reliability varied from city to city as local political and economic conditions changed, these statistical reports remain one of the most reliable sources for the study of crime and policing. The three series of reports used here contained a mixture of vital statistics, measures of economic performance, data on climate, and summaries of the actions of the police and judicial authorities.[5] The following analysis concentrates on one element of the police reports—arrests. Arrest data were generally presented in a uniform manner that facilitates comparison among these three cities. Other measures of criminal activity and police action, such as crimes reported by victims, the results of judicial action, and analyses of prison populations, are not examined here, because the data from the three cities were not reported in a similarly comparable format.

Arrest records do not permit the confident estimation of actual levels of criminal activity.[6] Since many crimes are not reported to the police, particularly rape, domestic assault, and petty theft, and because many criminals escape arrest, arrest records represent a fragment, albeit a large one, of total criminal activity. For Buenos Aires, the municipal statistical reports provide annual summaries of reported crimes, a valuable asset in estimating actual levels of criminal activity.[7] Since, however, the municipal authorities in Tucumán and Santa Fe did not provide these data, a systematic comparison of rates of reported crimes with arrests is not possible. The following analysis, therefore, concentrates on those topics where the weaknesses in arrest data are least troublesome—the identification of changes in police priorities and the establishment of trends and cycles in the arrest record. The relationship between these indices and the differences in economic structures and population characteristics among these three cities will also be analyzed. Beyond this, an effort will be made to evaluate the arrest experiences of these three Argentine cities in the light of theoretical expectations drawn from the study of crime in more developed societies.

The three cities to be examined were selected to represent distinct levels of political and economic development in pre-Depression Argentina. The dominant place of Buenos Aires in the economic and political order is well documented in the existing historical literature. Throughout this period, it was the undisputed national metropolis, directing the nation's political life and organizing the nation's economy.[8] With a population ten times larger than its nearest urban rival in 1914, it was one of the largest and most dynamic urban centers in the hemisphere. Santa Fe and Tucumán were provincial capitals with populations in 1930 of nearly equal size, approximately 130,000.[9] Table 1 provides population estimates for these three cities during an economically and demographically expansive period, 1895–1930. Although Santa Fe was substantially smaller than Tucumán before World War I, a boom in provincial agriculture, especially wheat production, propelled this city to near parity with Tucumán on the eve of the Great Depression. The growth of Santa Fe resulted primarily from its role as the key provincial administrative and banking center and from its function in regional commercial exchange.[10] The rapid expansion of wheat agriculture in the littoral drew tens of thousands of European immigrants to the province, and much of the city's population growth resulted from this flow. Although the province of Buenos Aires was the preeminent destination for immigrants to Argentina, the foreign-born component of Santa Fe's population remained above 30 percent to 1935.[11]

Tucumán also enjoyed a period of general economic prosperity and sustained population growth that began in the 1880s and lasted until 1906, when the sugar industry entered a decade of crisis. During the period of expansion, Tucumán experienced a series of economic and political changes occasioned by the increased power of refining interests relative to the traditionally dominant planter class. Although substantial new investments were made in all sectors of production, refining was the area where structural changes transformed existing social relationships most dramatically. In the countryside, production practices, land-tenure arrangements, and class relationships remained essentially unaltered until the eve of World War I. After 1914, both the number of large land-holdings owned by refineries and the number of minifundios increased.[12] Increased labor demands were met initially by the local use of compulsory-labor laws and later through migrant laborers recruited in neighboring provinces.[13] Bolivians were also

Table 1

Population of Buenos Aires, Santa Fe and Tucumán, 1900–30

Year	Buenos Aires	Santa Fe	Tucumán
1895	663,854	22,244	34,305
1900	815,680	27,982	58,290
1905	1,013,680	33,720	67,558
1910	1,306,680	44,834	78,696
1915	1,563,082	68,992	103,991
1920	1,629,016	85,323	108,804
1925	1,914,400	108,707	120,520
1930	2,254,400	122,151	133,334

Sources: for Buenos Aires Nicolas Moreno, *Buenos Aires. Puerto del Río de la Plata. Capital de la Argentina* (Buenos Aires, 1939), for Santa Fe Dirección de Estadística Municipal, *Anuario Estadístico de la Ciudad de Santa Fe* (Santa Fe, 1905–1931, Años i-vi, vols. viii-xxii; Provincia de Tucumán, *Anuario de Estadística* (Tucumán, 1900–1930).

recruited for harvest work, but numbers remained relatively low until after World War II. As a result, foreign nationals were never more othan 17 percent of the population of this provincial capital.[14] In sum, economic expansion in Tucumán occurred without fundamentally transforming the vestigial elements of the traditional creole social order.

In the analysis that follows, misdemeanor arrests and arrests for two categories of felony crime, crimes against persons and crimes against property, will be examined. In addition to these aggregate arrest categories, homicides and suicides will be analyzed. Existing theory derived from the study of European and North American cities suggests that the combined effects of urbanization and industrialization in the late nineteenth and twentieth centuries lowered the arrest rates for both misdemeanor and personal felony crimes. In response to this same process of social and economic change, arrest rates for felony property crime increased significantly in Europe and North America. Homicides, a subcategory of personal felony crime, generally declined at a rate similar to that found for all violent crime.[15] This trend is now reversed in the United States, where homicides are rising to previously unknown levels. Suicide rates, on the other hand, generally moved in an inverse manner to the homicide rate, increasing during the process of economic development.[16]

Modernization is an obviously slippery concept that is highly vulnerable to abuse. In criminological analysis, it is used to subsume a broad range of economic and social indicators that include lowered birth and death rates, increased literacy levels, improving per capita and household income levels, and a proportional increase in the size of both the manufacturing work force and the public sector. Accepting the definitional weakness of modernization, it is still possible to assert confidently a socioeconomic rank order for these Argentine cities. Buenos Aires most closely approximated the experience of the rapidly growing cities of North America. Tucumán, on the other hand, maintained characteristics of its preindustrial past. Evidence to justify this hierarchy can be extracted from contemporary censuses and other government publications.

By the early 1930s, the crude birth and death rates for Buenos Aires and Santa Fe were approaching those found in most cities of contemporary Europe. Although both Argentine cities had relatively high crude birth rates on the eve of World War I, these rates had fallen to twenty per thousand in 1930. By comparison, Tucumán maintained a consistently high crude birth rate of at least forty-two per thousand well into the Depression decade. This birth rate was much closer to that found for Bolivia or Peru than to the rates of the other two Argentine cities examined here. Crude death rates provide a similar patttern. In 1935, Buenos Aires and Santa Fe had crude death rates of eleven per thousand while Tucumán registered twenty-five per thousand.[17]

Other social indicators support the rank order derived from vital statistics. In the censuses of 1895 and 1914, Tucumán had proportionally twice as many illiterates as the other two cities. The city of Buenos Aires had, of course, the highest literacy rate in Latin America. Santa Fe, also benefitting from the arrival of large numbers of literate foreigners, had an effective adult literacy of more than 80 percent. This hierarchy remains clear, even in provincial-level distributions of hearing- and speech-impaired residents provided in contemporary censuses. Proportionally, Tucumán had three times as many cases of hearing and speech impairment as Santa Fe. Buenos Aires, on the other hand, had approximately 20 percent fewer hearing- and speech-impaired residents than Santa Fe.[18] Fragments of per capita and household income data are also in agreement with the rank order suggested by these indices.[19] If criminological theory adequately explains the Argentine case, we should expect that the arrest rates for Buenos Aires would most closely approximate the rates established for more developed nations while Tucumán should diverge most visibly. The arrest rates for Santa Fe should fall between those found for the other two cities and be moving in the direction of Buenos Aires during this period.

The record of misdemeanor arrests offers a fascinating, but difficult to interpret, area for investigation. These infractions include public drunkenness, disorderly conduct, the carrying of weapons, and other forms of public nuisance. In every modern city studied so far, public drunkenness was the most common misdemeanor offense. Disorderly-conduct arrests, the next largest category, seldom exceeded 40 percent of arrests for drunkenness. Weapons charges and all other nonfelony infractions commonly contribute less than 10 percent of total misdemeanor arrests. In Argentina, and generally in the Western Hemisphere and in Europe, misdemeanor arrests result from the initiative of an individual police officer and do not require either a formal complaint by a victim or a judicial order.[20] Because of the broad discretionary power provided to the police in these cases, it must be presumed that substantial changes in the annual number of misdemeanor arrests tended to reflect changed police priorities as well as actual alterations in public conduct. A major contributor to this process was the diversion of police manpower away from patrol functions to criminal investigations and tasks as diverse as the supervision of building codes and the care of lost children.[21]

Graph 1 illustrates misdemeanor-arrest rates, misdemeanor arrests per thousand inhabitants, in these three Argentine cities during the period 1900–30. Rates rather than actual arrests are used throughout this analysis to control for differences in population size among the three cities and within each city over time. Because arrest data were not published for Santa Fe before 1904, and the statistical department of Buenos Aires ignored arrests for misdemeanors from 1915 through 1918, estimated rates for these years were interpolated for this graph. Although there were obvious differences in enforcement practices among these three cities, the actual offenses included in this aggregate arrest category remained identical throughout the period.

Studies of European and North American cities demonstrate that arrests for public-order offenses declined during the late nineteenth century. The modern commercial-industrial city transformed urban culture by imposing on its residents the discipline of the factory whistle, timecard, and assembly line. Closely supervised labor and the six-day work week reduced the free time available for drinking, casual socializing in the streets, and other activities that serve commonly as venues for disorderliness and masculine violence. Higher literacy levels, expanded public education, improved housing opportunities, and the development of a uniformed police force also promoted a more orderly public.[22] In a recently published study of twenty-three cities in the United States, Eric Monkkonen concluded that "the actual incidence of disorderly conduct in public decreased," during the period from 1860 to 1980.[23] This argument is supported by convincing evidence from contemporary sources in the United States and Europe. Since, however, misdemeanor arrests provide the only continuous record for measuring levels of public order, it is virtually impossible to separate the effects of changed police practice from the long-term effects of cultural change. These problems also obstruct the effort to understand the Argentine experience.

The decline in the misdemeanor-arrest rate found for Buenos Aires parallels that of North American cities during this same period. Public-order arrests in Buenos Aires trended downward to 1930 with the exception of a brief period, 1911–13, when the rate moved abruptly upward. This increase in misdemeanor arrests followed a period of violent labor agitation that began in 1909 with a general strike and the assassination of the metropolitan police chief. In 1910, anarchist leaders threatened to disrupt the centennial celebrations of independence. A violent cycle of right-wing vigilante actions, antisemitic attacks, and left-wing responses that included the bombing of the Colón Theater followed. Yet, by 1914, the gradual downward trend in misdemeanor arrests was reestablished.

Graph 1
Misdemeanor Arrest Rate for Three Argentine Cities

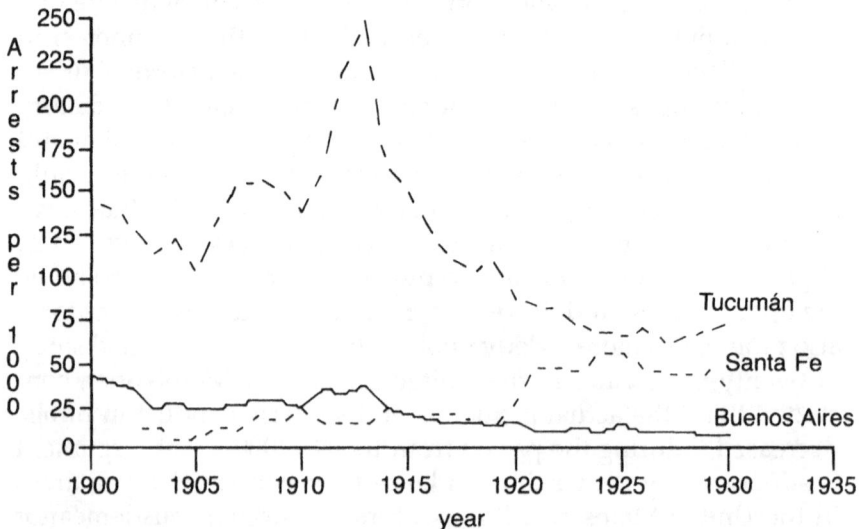

This overall decline in misdemeanor arrests in Argentina's capital city was the continuation of a long-term process that began in the mid-1880s. The misdemeanor-arrest rate fell precipitously from 1880 to 1890, then leveled off and continued gradually declining until the beginning of the twentieth century.[24] By 1920, the misdemeanor rate for Buenos Aires was actually lower than the rates found in cities of a similar size in the United States.[25] It is particularly important to remember that this decline in public-order arrests occurred during a tumultuous political period and coincided with two serious economic recessions. Clearly, the forces that were driving the misdemeanor rate downward were not easily disrupted by extraneous events, even when these events were capable of reversing trans-Atlantic migration flows and overturning the national government.

The data for Buenos Aires are compatible with explanations that emphasize both changed enforcement practice and altered public behavior. Published studies of the city's police department provide overwhelming evidence that police resources were increasingly diverted from the maintenance of public order to new tasks. Chief among these additional functions was the apprehension of criminals guilty of felony crimes. By 1914, the Buenos Aires police department had developed the full range of modern crime-fighting functions. Police publications from the period proudly describe new mobile patrols, crime labs, a detective branch, and new recruitment and training practices.[26] These services and responsibilities necessarily reduced the number and frequency of neighborhood foot patrols as manpower was reassigned. Fewer officers walking the beat resulted in fewer discretionary arrests. In addition to these changes in police manning priorities, increased levels of political violence after 1895 forced municipal authorities in Buenos Aires to allocate police resources to the protection of public officials and government buildings.[27]

Changes in residential patterns and in the scale of immigration to Argentina also influenced misdemeanor-arrest levels in Buenos Aires. The development of new suburban housing precincts after 1900 promoted greater residential segregation and thereby reduced the likelihood of violence between ethnic groups.[28] Improvements in the housing stock also contributed to public order by allowing greater numbers of the urban working class to socialize indoors away from police scrutiny. These changes in housing patterns coincided with a reduction in the flow of immigrants from Europe. During World War I, Argentina actually experienced a net outmigration of nearly a quarter of a million men and women.[29] A less visible immigrant population in the city's business center diminished public fears of disorder and violence and provided an opportunity for municipal authorities to redirect police resources away from social-control duties to the prevention and punishment of serious crime.

It is difficult to shed much light on the misdemeanor-arrest patterns for the other two cities with existing theory. Tucumán's arrest rate for public-order offenses presents a different order of magnitude, although the overall trend and the periodization of changes are somewhat similar to those found for Buenos Aires. Throughout the entire period, the misdemeanor rate in Tucumán was at least six times higher than the rate in the capital city. In fact, the peak rate of 248 per 1000 inhabitants recorded in 1913 was more than twice as high as the peak rate established in Buenos Aires in 1888. Both the number of arrests for a city of this size (potentially one in four residents of Tucumán experienced a misdemeanor arrest in 1913) and the volatility of the arrest rate during this thirty-one-year period are striking.[30] Since neither drinking habits nor the inclination to boisterousness and public rowdiness are readily altered in a stable population, annual swings of between 15 and 65 percent in the misdemeanor-arrest rate must have resulted in part from changed police priorities in this provincial capital.

Despite the huge increase in arrests in the years before World War I, the overall pattern in Tucumán might be viewed as the early stage of the declining trend in misdemeanor arrests found for Buenos Aires and many North American cities. Before this hypothesis can be accepted, misdemeanor rates for the 1940s and 1950s must be calculated to discover if this decline continued or was a short-term anomaly. Even if Tucumán was moving in the direction predicted by theory, the violent cyclical swings in public-order arrests require an effort at explanation. The dramatically increased arrest rates for the period 1907–13 coincided with a general crisis in the sugar industry that was induced by a deterioration in local cane stock and by changes in the export market.[31] Because this crisis affected the agricultural, rather than the refining, side of sugar production, it provoked a major disruption in regional employment levels and forced large numbers of rural workers into the provincial capital to look for alternative employment. In contrast, a massive strike among urban refinery workers in 1923 did not provoke an increase in misdemeanor arrests, although the *cañeros* strike of 1927 did produce a slight increase in arrests for disorderly conduct.[32] In this case, the cultural explanation serves us best. In the early crisis, the arrival of large numbers of displaced rural workers, unaccustomed to the social practices and behavioral norms of the city, drove up the level of public-order arrests. Strike activity by urban workers in 1923 and by cane farmers in 1927, however, had a reduced effect.

Santa Fe presents even greater interpretive problems. Data for the period 1902–30 indicate an upward trend in misdemeanor arrests. This upward movement increased substantially in strength during the last decade before the Depression, a period when the city made great progress in socioeconomic terms.[33] This was also a time when efforts to modernize the police force were undertaken, although the department in Santa Fe continued to lag behind Buenos Aires in developing modern crime-fighting functions.

There were two peaks in the misdemeanor rate for Santa Fe. The first coincided with World War I. During the four-year period from 1914 to 1917, the city experienced a misdemeanor-arrest rate of twenty-two per thousand. The second, and more important, period of increased arrests occurred during the last decade before the Depression (an annual average of forty-eight arrests per thousand inhabitants). Peak years during this decade were 1924–25, when police made fifty-seven misdemeanor arrests per thousand inhabitants. Both periods of increased public-order arrests coincided with contractions in the provincial economy. The period of World War I produced the greatest difficulties for the commercial farmers and grain processors of Santa Fe. Although the effects were much reduced, provincial agriculture also confronted a second, and much less severe, period of adjustment in the mid-1920s as international demand declined.[34]

In both periods of agricultural contraction, thousands of rural workers were compelled to seek alternative employment in the region's cities. Confronted with large numbers of young men, few of them accustomed to urban life, the police used misdemeanor arrests to discipline these new residents. The arrest rate was lower in the earlier period, even though the economic downturn was more serious, because large numbers of displaced rural workers returned to Europe to participate in World War I. During the 1920s, the social consequences of the economic contraction were exacerbated by changes in land-tenure arrangements that pushed the sons of tenants as well as laborers off the land.

Arrests for serious crimes, felonies, offer the researcher a more reliable index of changes in actual levels of criminal behavior. Whereas misdemeanor arrests commonly resulted from police initiative, felony arrests seldom occurred without a formal complaint by a victim or a police investigation. Because felony arrests could only be cleared after official judicial scrutiny, the police were much less likely in these cases to make frivolous or unwarranted arrests. Changes in felony-arrest levels, therefore, were more closely linked to actual fluctuations in criminal activity. This is not to say that felony arrests can be used to represent the universe of criminal acts. In any society, arrests are necessarily less numerous than criminal acts. Many victims fail to report crimes, and the police do not clear many cases through arrests.[35]

In the following analysis, arrests for two aggregate categories of felony crime will be examined, crimes against persons (also identified as violent crimes in this discussion) and crimes against property. Crimes against persons were typically either simple or aggravated assaults. This category also includes homicides, abortions, and manslaughter. Thefts and robberies were the most common property crimes. Because the victims of crimes against persons could often identify their assailants, a high percentage of these complaints were cleared by an arrest. A much smaller percentage of felony property crimes reported to the police were cleared through arrest. Currently in the United States, the clearance rate for property crimes is roughly 50 percent of the personal-crime clearance rate.[36] Therefore, it may be assumed that the arrest rates for personal crime in these three Argentine cities were much closer to the actual levels of criminal activity than were the arrest rates for property crime.

The literature on crime in the United States and Europe suggest that the arrest rate for property crime should increase relative to the arrest rate for violent crime during the process of urbanization and industrialization. In the developed world today, 82 percent of all reported offenses are property crimes, theft being the most common.[37] Among the many circumstances that influenced this trend were the greater availability of an emphasis on material goods, the impersonality of city life, and the reduced supervision of juveniles by parents tied to more rigid urban work schedules.

Graph 2 illustrates felony-arrest rates for Buenos Aires. The picture presented is an ambiguous one. There were two periods when felony arrests moved in expected directions. In the first three years of this century, arrests for property crimes moved sharply upward, while violent crimes declined slightly. No clear upward trend, however, emerged until 1913. A high level of property-crime arrests was maintained from this date until 1921. In 1919, there were 261 arrests for property crimes for every 100 arrests for violent crime in the city of Buenos Aires. The final decade before the Depression witnessed the inversion of this relationship. Arrests for property crimes fell, while those for violent crimes pushed upward. Between 1926 and 1930, there were only 46 arrests for property crime for every 100 arrests for violent crime.

In these three decades, there is no clear trend in arrests for violent crimes, although three cyclical declines occurred. The arrest

Graph 2
Felony Arrest Rates for Buenos Aires

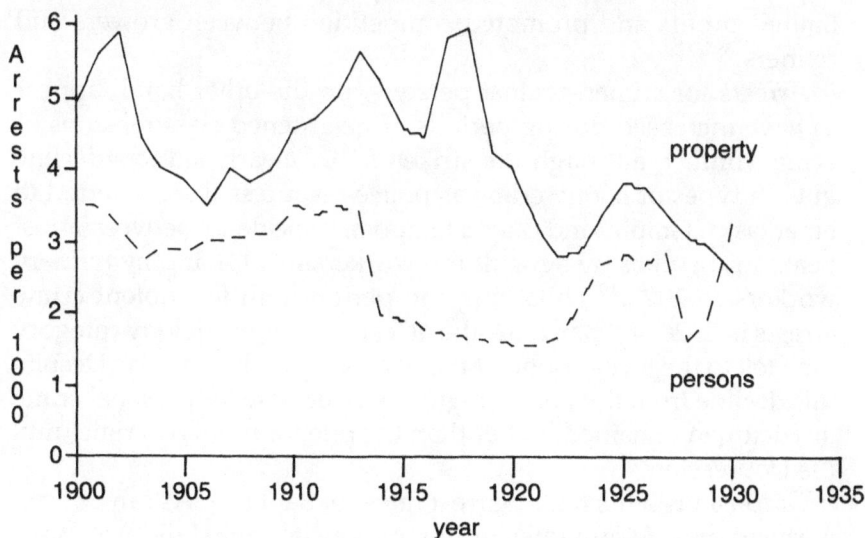

rate for property crime actually tended downward. Since the literature suggests that property crimes should increase during modernization, the decline in this rate in Buenos Aires is especially surprising, given the city's overall prosperity and economic progress during these years. There were, however, increases in felony property crime during two periods of economic contraction, 1900–1903 and 1915–18. The connection between violent crime and class and political conflict was ambiguous. The increased rate of violent crime arrests in 1929 and 1930 may have been linked to the overthrow of Hipólito Yrigoyen and the imposition of military rule. It is important to note, though, that arrests for violent crime actually declined in 1919, the year of the *Semana Trágica*.[38]

As was the case with misdemeanor arrests, both felony-arrest rates for Tucumán fluctuated broadly without any clear trend emerging. There is certainly no evidence that arrests for violent crime were declining relative to property crime during this period. The lowest rates for property-crime arrests coincided with a generalized crisis in the sugar industry, 1904–13. As in the Buenos Aires case, peak years for the property-crime arrest rate occurred during the war years as the economy adjusted to dramatically altered market conditions. By the early 1920s, provincial planters had successfully introduced a new variety of cane and production increased impressively. The international collapse in sugar prices, however, limited profits and promoted competition between growers and refiners.[39]

Arrests for crimes against persons, on the other hand, appear to have increased during periods of heightened class tensions or actual conflict, although the strike of 1927 clearly led to a decline in both types of felony crime as police resources were diverted to other tasks. Graph 3 indicates a temporal coincidence between arrest peaks and strikes by agricultural workers in 1904 and by refinery workers in 1923.[40] Following the period high for violent crime arrests in 1926, 4.8 per 1000, the arrest rate for this felony category then fell to the levels found at the beginning of the century. Despite this decline from the period high, the arrest rate for personal crime in Tucumán remained higher than the rate for property crime until the Depression.

Graph 4 presents felony-arrest rates for Santa Fe. As can be seen in this graph, felony rates in this provincial capital did not move

Graph 3
Felony Arrest Rate for Tucumán

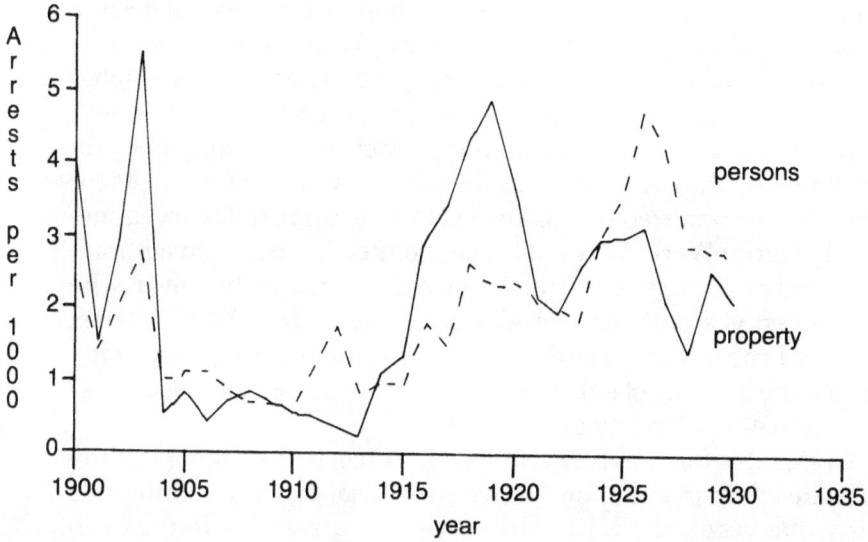

Graph 4
Felony Arrest Rate for Santa Fe

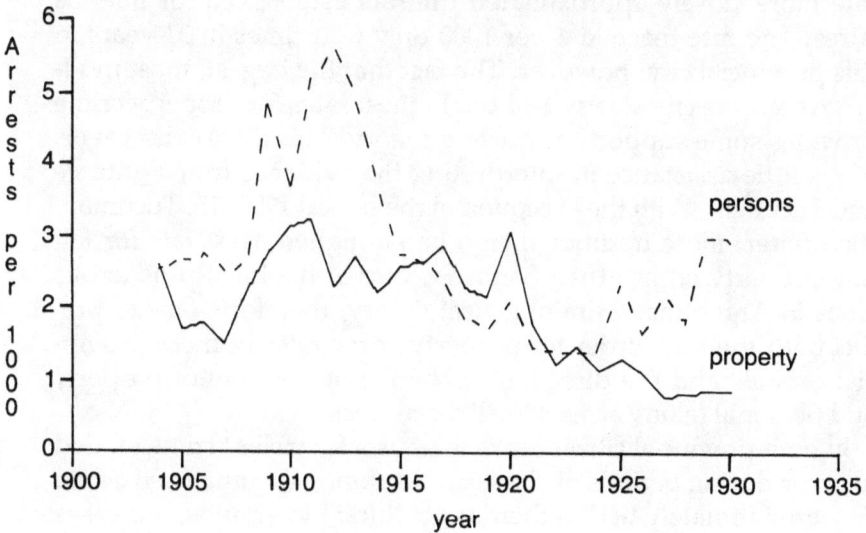

in the direction predicted by theory. In fact, arrest data from Santa Fe diverge further from existing theory than do the data from the more traditional city of Tucumán. Although some cyclical increases in property crime occurred after 1900, there was an overall decline in this arrest category during the 1920s. In fact, there were only eight years when arrests in Santa Fe for property crimes were higher than for violent crimes. The theoretical expectation that violent crimes would decline relative to property crimes is simply not substantiated by the evidence from this city. Peak years for arrests for violent crime occurred during the years of agrarian militancy immediately before World War I. No clear connection between agrarian problems and levels of urban violence can be made, however. The final seven years of the period were characterized by low arrest rates for property crime and a steeply increasing violent-crime rate, despite the absence of substantial levels of political violence or class conflict in either the city or province.

Arrest rates for property crime were consistently higher in Buenos Aires than in either of the two provincial capitals. During this thirty-one-year period, the property-crime arrest rate in the capital city only fell below 4 arrests per 1000 inhabitants ten times. In comparison, Santa Fe's peak rate was 3.2 arrests per 1000 in 1911. During the period 1921–30, the arrest rate for property crimes in this city failed to reach 2 per 1000. Tucumán's property-crime arrest rate more closely approximated the rate established for Buenos Aires. The rate reached 4 per 1000 only four times in 31 years in this provincial city, however. The fact that the largest, most modern Argentine city clearly had the highest rates for property crime provides some support for existing theory. This theory, however, offers little assistance in interpreting the evidence from Santa Fe and Tucumán. With the exception of the period 1904–15, Tucumán, the poorer, more traditional city, had a higher arrest rate for felony property crimes than Santa Fe, one of the most prosperous cities in Argentina. Criminological theory, therefore, fails to predict both the rank order for property-crime rates in these provincial capitals and the direction of change in the ratio of property and personal felony arrests in all three cities.

In both provincial cities, peaks in arrests for violent crime tended to occur during periods of class conflict. Since Tucumán and Santa Fe were intimately tied to their agricultural hinterlands, increases in arrests for violent crime in these cities often coincided with rural conflicts, as well as with urban strikes and political instability. The relationship between arrests for violent crime and class conflict is less clear in Buenos Aires. Changes in the arrest rate for violent crime in Buenos Aires were not closely associated with strikes or political conflict, except for the years 1910–13 and 1929–30. Arrests for crimes against persons actually fell in 1919, the year of the *Semana Trágica*. There was no apparent connection between labor conflict in the province of Buenos Aires and city arrest levels. Although no firm conclusions can be drawn at this point, it appears that the capital's more diversified economy, especially the ability of municipal and national authorities to employ large numbers of men and women and distribute social services, operated to limit and control the effects of class conflict.

Both Buenos Aires and Santa Fe experienced a decline in the arrest rate for crimes against persons during World War I. This was a period when there was a net outmigration of approximately 250,000 foreign nationals from Argentina. Beginning in 1914, when 61,103 immigrants returned to Europe from Argentina, this demographic hemorrhage persisted until 1919. The coincidence of this change in international migration flows and the decline in arrests for violent crime in two cities with large immigrant populations suggests that in Argentina interpersonal violence was disproportionally concentrated in this sector of the urban population. It is not clear that the immigrants were more violent than the native-born population, however. The marginally higher arrest rates found for immigrants may have been simply the result of proportionally larger numbers of unmarried, young males among the foreign-born.[41]

Homicide arrests were a small, but important, component of the felony category crimes against persons. It is the arrest category that most closely approximates the universe of actual criminal acts, since a very high percentage of these crimes are cleared by arrest. The literature suggests that in the period before World War II, rural areas were generally more violent, more murderous, than urban centers. That is, more rural, traditional places, like Tucumán, generally had higher homicide rates than did more economically diversified and socially complex cities, like Buenos Aires and Santa Fe.[42] In the years since 1945, this pattern has been dramatically altered by the appearance of staggeringly high homicide rates in large U.S.

and Third World cities.[43] By the standard of contemporary urban America, pre-Depression Argentina was a remarkably peaceful society. Yet, violent deaths were common enough to provoke widespread concern among experts and in the popular press.[44] Graph 5 presents homicide-arrest rates for these three Argentine cities. In this graph, the rate is calculated as incidents per ten thousand inhabitants in order to more effectively display the results.

The reader can see immediately that throughout this thirty-one-year period, the homicide rate for Buenos Aires was much higher than the rates found for the other two cities. In all three cities we find some examples of substantial short-term fluctuations in homicide rates. Buenos Aires from 1900 to 1904, Santa Fe from 1913 to 1916, and Tucumán from 1917 to 1920 are examples of this phenomenon. The causes for these fluctuations are, however, difficult to pinpoint. Some periods when political conflict and strike activity were associated temporally with an increase in homicides can be isolated. For example, the widespread labor unrest of 1919–20 coincided with an increase in homicide-arrest rates calculated for

Graph 5
Homicide Rate for Three Argentine Cities

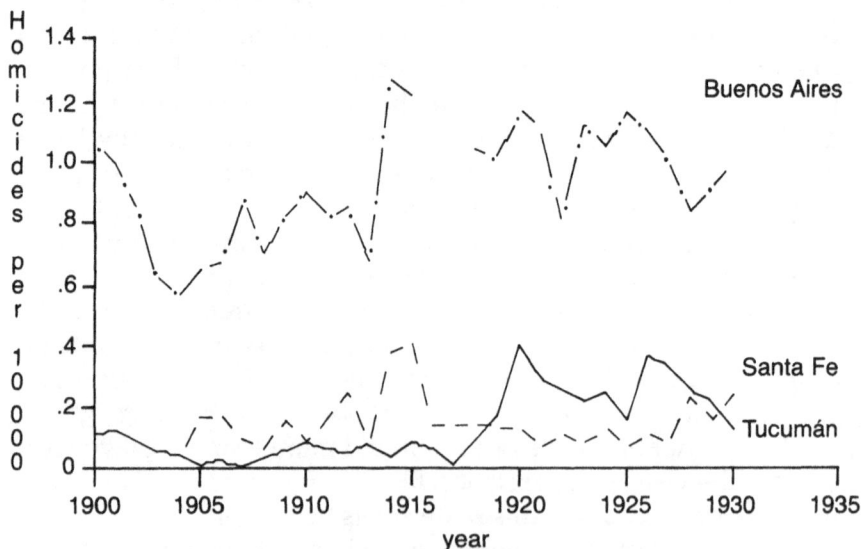

both Buenos Aires and Tucumán. Yet, Santa Fe actually experienced a slight decline in this rate during the same period. The collapse of the Yrigoyen government in 1929, conversely, was contemporaneous with a decline in homicide arests in Buenos Aires and Tucumán and an increase in Santa Fe. Although these coincidences are interesting, the evidence does not permit us to argue a clear association between homicide-arrest rates and economic performance, class tensions, or political conflict in Argentina.

There was no apparent connection between homicide-arrest rates and changes in the rate of urban or provincial population growth. Dramatic increases, or decreases, in immigration did not coincide with significant changes in homicide arrests. This suggests that, in general, homicides and other types of violent crime were committed by two distinct populations. Assaults and other common forms of interpersonal violence were typically committed by unmarried laborers, often immigrants or native-born migrants.[45] This was the social sector least constrained by familial and material obligations, a population inclined to violently defend personal honor.[46] Murderers, on the other hand, were drawn from a more settled sector of the urban population.[47] Since the victim and perpetrator in homicide cases were commonly linked by kinship or other formal association, the outflow of young, unattached immigrants during the war years would have little effect on the homicide arrest rate.

With careful research it may be possible to link differences in homicide levels among these cities to differences in built environments and population densities. It can confidently be asserted that throughout this period the working class of Buenos Aires was housed in more crowded and unhygenic conditions than were found in either Santa Fe or Tucumán.[48] It may be that housing conditions were more important in determining homicide rates than were other circumstances, such as changes in per capita income, unemployment levels, or ethnic composition.[49] That is, the quality of material life and the architectural context for social interaction may more effectively illuminate the causes of interpersonal violence than additional work with gross measures of economic well-being.

Table 2 provides homicide and suicide rates for Buenos Aires and Tucumán for the twelve-year period 1919–30. Unfortunately, suicide data were not included in the municipal reports of Santa

Table 2
Homicide and Suicide Rates for Buenos Aires and Tucumán,
1919–1930.

| | Rates per 10,000 | | | |
| | Buenos Aires | | Tucumán | |
	Homicide	Suicide	Homicide	Suicide
1919	1.02	1.32	.18	1.12
1920	1.16	1.21	.40	1.28
1921	1.12	1.29	.30	1.18
1922	.81	1.30	.26	1.15
1923	1.12	1.45	.22	1.38
1924	1.05	1.63	.25	.85
1925	1.16	1.81	.17	1.57
1926	1.10	2.12	.37	2.20
1927	1.00	2.23	.34	1.99
1928	.84	2.55	.26	1.56
1929	.77	2.63	.22	2.07
1930	.76	2.48	.14	2.10

Fe. In examining this table, both a wide discrepancy in homicide rates and a close similarity in suicide rates are found. Although no systematic study is available, it appears that the rate of violent crime, both homicides and assaults, has risen dramatically in Tucumán since 1930. In 1953, Tucumán actually experienced more assaults and homicides than Buenos Aires, a city with a population seven times larger.[50] That is, the post-World War II data from Argentina seem to provide some evidence for the theoretical expectation that this form of violent crime declines in response to urbanization and industrialization. This trend, however, is not visible during the thirty years studied here.

As discussed earlier, the homicide rate for Buenos Aires was high throughout the first three decades of the century, although it remained slightly lower than contemporary homicide rates established for industrial cities in the United States. The rate of the Argentine capital was, however, higher than the rate found in major Spanish and Italian cities.[51] Since cultural differences between these European cities and Buenos Aires were minimal, the higher homicide rate in the Argentine capital is probably best explained by the greater proportion of young males in its population. It was this special feature of immigration, the expansion of the demographic cohort that provided most of both murderers and victims, that best explains the capital city's high homicide rate.[52]

After 1925, both Argentine cities produced suicide rates that were substantially higher than those found elsewhere in the hemisphere.[53] A brief survey of some comparative data will help put these suicide rates in perspective. In Philadelphia in 1890, the rate for native-born Americans was .50 per 10,000. Foreign-born residents generally had slightly higher rates. Italian and Irish immigrants had rates of .64 and .53 per 10,000, respectively. Only two immigrant groups in Philadelphia had suicide rates similar to the overall rates found in these two Argentine cities, Bohemians and Hungarians.[54] During the decade 1910–20, Chicago produced a suicide rate of 1.20 for the native-born and 3.27 for all foreign-born residents. Philadelphia during this same period had a suicide rate of 1.07 for the native-born and 2.31 for the foreign-born. The suicide rates for the foreign-born residents of these two North American cities are misleading, however. This aggregate statistic disguises broad differences among various immigrant groups. Germans, Austrians, Hungarians, and Scandinavians had very high suicide rates, often higher than 3.5 per 10,000. Italian and Spanish immigrants in the cities of the United States had the lowest rates among the foreign-born.[55] Since the immigrant population in Argentina was overwhelmingly drawn from these two populations, we should expect that the rate for Buenos Aires would fall in the range between the North American rates for the native-born and immigrants from Spain and Italy.

Instead, the suicide rate for Buenos Aires pushed upward even after the peak years of immigration, producing an average rate of 2.30 per 10,000 for the period 1925–30. Tucumán, with an insignificant foreign-born population, imitated the rising rates of the capital city, establishing an average rate of 1.92 for the last six years of this period. Could these rates be one measure of the human costs imposed by the economic contraction that followed the war? Research suggests that there is a relationship between economic cycles and the suicide rate. These studies indicate that the suicide rate generally tends to increase during economic recessions. During the early period of an economic recovery, rates also tend to increase, although not as dramatically.[56] The movement of the suicide rates from these two cities appears to fit this theoretical expectation. Rates for the depression decade in Argentina, however, will have to be calculated before this relationship can be confidently asserted. It is worth recalling that at the height of the depression in the United States, the suicide rate was 1.86, 25 percent lower than the rate in Buenos Aires in 1930.[57]

Could the data from Argentina be artificially inflated? Were substantial numbers of accidental deaths or homicides classified as suicides by the authorities of Tucumán and Buenos Aires? Because of the Catholic church's strong proscriptions against suicide, it is much more likely that local authorities would deflate the numbers by classifying possible suicides as accidental deaths. Unless the evidence of suicide was irrefutable, the families of decedents would seek to avoid notoriety and scandal by pressuring the police to use the accidental-death category. It seems safe to presume, therefore, that the rate presented in Table 2 is based on an underestimation, rather than an overestimation, of deaths by suicide.

Although suicide and homicide are commonly linked in scholarly inquiry, these are acts perpetrated by different populations. Both suicide and homicide are acts of violent aggression most commonly committed by males, although attempted suicides do not show this same sex bias.[58] In societies with stable populations, suicides are disproportionally drawn from more privileged classes. Murderers and their victims are generally members of the working class. In societies with large numbers of immigrants or internal migrants, these class characteristics of suicide are less clear. Both of these high-risk groups, the privileged and immigrants, share some social characteristics that appear to promote higher suicide rates: a low level of social restraint (the effect of limited relationships with other persons) and a low level of truly collective activity (the degree of involvement in group relationships).

In the nineteenth century, students of violent death first identified a marginally higher suicide rate among immigrants. Émile Durkheim associated this form of suicide with the condition of anomie, being separated from traditional associations, values, and routines. The powerful, disorienting feelings of alienation and loneliness are more likely experienced by immigrants, particularly young, unmarried males, than by the native-born population. The high suicide rate found for Buenos Aires, the preeminent immigrant city of the Americas, appears to confirm this association. It should be expected that Santa Fe experienced similar levels of suicide during the period of immigration. What about Tucumán, a traditional creole city with a very small immigrant population? It is important to remember in this context that Tucumán was also a city with a large population of migrants coming from the countryside, from neighboring provinces, and from Bolivia.[59] These migrants experienced adjustment problems that were essentially similar to those affecting Italian and other European immigrants living in the national capital.

It was not only the foreignness (cultural distinctiveness) of immigrants that promoted isolation and the personal despair that led to suicide, although problems of cultural adjustment limited an immigrant's opportunities to forge the network of social ties that reduce the likelihood of suicide. Cut off from traditional surroundings and deprived of contact with family and close friends, native-born migrants and immigrants from Europe shared a social and emotional environment that offered little support during moments of personal crisis. These inherent features of the immigrant condition in Argentina were exacerbated by the frustrations and sense of personal failure that accompanied the periods of high unemployment and low wages that were built into an economy dominated by the violent swings of the export market. Although wages were generally higher in Argentina than in Europe, there was little investment in skills, and nearly all the work force, both rural and urban, was affected immediately by changes in export demand. As a result, each contraction set thousands of men and women in motion looking for employment. Movement was survival. In these conditions, the ability of immigrants to establish roots and build the interpersonal relationships that reduce the likelihood of suicide were much reduced. In this melancholy statistic, then, may reside the best index for measuring the social costs of Argentina's economic transformation.

This combination of circumstances, the presence of large numbers of immigrants and migrants, the volatility of the economy, and the resulting fluidity of the population, also influenced the relatively high levels of arrests for public-order misdemeanors and felony crimes against persons. The Argentine urban working class was less settled than similar classes in the industrial centers of

Europe and North America. A relatively larger group of young, unmarried males living away from the controlling influences of family and long-standing friendships is much more likely to produce high arrest indices for violence and disorder. Cyclical contractions of the agricultural economy, the ongoing crisis in Tucumán's sugar industry for example, not only produced angry protest, but also exacerbated social isolation by hindering the ability of workers to establish and sustain families. In Tucumán in 1913, 70 percent of adult internal migrants were unmarried. Similarly high levels are found for internal and international migrants in Buenos Aires and Santa Fe.

Arrest records from these three Argentine cities raise some serious questions about the relationship between crime and policing and the modernization process. It is clear that these three cities do not neatly fit theoretical expectations developed from the historical experiences of the United States and Europe. These analytical problems are most likely the result of weaknesses in the concept of modernization. There can be no doubt that after 1880 Argentina entered a long period of dynamic economic expansion. By 1930, wage and income levels in the littoral compared favorably with those found in many European nations.[60] The effects of an expanded public-school system and the continued flow of literate immigrants improved the general cultural level and provided the factual basis for the common *porteño* boast that Argentina is not a part of Latin America. Finally, by 1914, the national housing crisis was largely overcome. Throughout Argentina, urban residents were living lives that compared favorably in material terms with those of contemporaries in Europe or North America. Yet, these similarities in a broad range of socioeconomic variables tended to disguise, rather than illuminate, the nature of Argentine economic development. Profound structural differences distinguished the Argentine economy from the economies of developed nations.

The export-led economic development of Argentina failed to provide stable employment for all but a tiny fraction of the working class. Throughout this long period of relative prosperity, the Argentine work force remained extremely fluid, even in the urban service sector, and in manufacturing there was little stable employment. This characteristic has been identified before in studies of Buenos Aires during the era of immigration. The instability of employment and the resulting fluidity of the working class in the interior has, however, been largely ignored. By weakening social bonds and creating a highly mobile subculture of young, unskilled males, this feature of Argentina's development process promoted the continuation of high levels of violent crime, despite the broad expansion of modern material culture. The complex effects of a stratification system rooted in this form of economic development also provided the social context for the rising suicide rates found for Tucumán and Buenos Aires in the 1920s. These connections between economic change and various measures of criminal acitivity cannot be demonstrated conclusively until new research on work-force distribution, employment persistence, and police practice is undertaken. Although the pursuit of these research objectives will be difficult, the field offers a unique opportunity to explore the underside of social change.

Notes

1. This is not the place to review the entire literature on crime and policing. It is, however, important to acknowledge a representative cross section of the more notable contributions. William B. Taylor's *Drinking, Homicide and Rebellion in Colonial Mexican Villages* (Stanford, 1979) remains one of the most original and interesting studies of crime and social deviancy in Latin America. Two other worthwhile studies of the colonial period are Susan M. Socolow, "Women and Crime: Buenos Aires, 1757–97," *Journal of Latin American Studies* (May 1980): 39–54; and Colin MacLachlan, *Criminal Justice in Eighteenth Century Mexico: A Study of the Tribunal of the Acordada* (Berkeley, 1974). Relative to other Latin American nations, Mexico and Brazil have attracted substantial scholarly attention. Among the many valuable contributions are: Martha Knisely Huggins, *From Slavery to Vagrancy in Brazil* (New Brunswick, 1985); Patricia Ann Aufderheide, "Order and Violence: Social Deviance and Social Control in Brazil, 1780–1840," Ph.D. dissertation, University of Minnesota, 1975; Boris Fausto, *Crime e cotidiano: A criminalidade em São Paulo 1880–1924* (São Paulo, 1984); Paul J. Vanderwood, *Disorder and Progress. Bandits, Police, and Mexican Development* (Lincoln: 1981); Laurence J. Rohlfes, "Police and Penal Correction in Mexico City, 1876–1911: A Study of Order and Progress in Porfirian Mexico," Ph.D. dissertation, Tulane University, 1983. For an interesting collection of essays on banditry, see *Bibliotheca Americana* vol. 1 No. 2 (Nov., 1982).

2. A good general survey of this topic is provided in Louise I. Shelley, *Crime and Modernization: The Impact of Industrialization and Urbanization on Crime* (Carbondale, 1981). See also Ted Robert Gurr and Peter N. Grabosky, *Rogues, Rebels, and Reformers: A Political History of Urban Crime and Conflict* (Beverly Hills, 1976).

3. Among the many fine studies of crime and policing in modern cities, are: Eric H. Monkkonen, *Police in Urban American, 1860–1920* (Cambridge, Mass., 1981); David Jones, *Crime, Protest, Community, and Police in Nineteenth-Century Britain* (London, 1982); Roger Lane, *Violent Death in the City: Suicide, Accident, and Murder in 19th Century Philadelphia* (Cambridge, Mass., 1979); John C. Schneider, *Detroit and the Problem of Order, 1830–1880: A Geography of Crime, Riot, and Policing* (Lincoln, 1980); and Lawrence M. Friedman and Robert V. Percival, *The Roots of Justice: Crime and Punishment in Alameda County, California, 1870–1910* (Chapel Hill, N.C., 1981).

4. Eric H. Monkkonen, "Municipal Reports as an Indicator Source: The Nineteenth-Century Police," *Historical Methods* (Spring 1979): 57–65, provides a good survey of this source. See his "Systematic Criminal Justice History: Some Suggestions," *Journal of Interdisciplinary History* (Winter, 1979): 451–64. Another helpful contribution is found in Donald J. Black, "Production of Crime Rates," *American Sociological Review* (Aug. 1980): 733–48. For an example of the usefulness of these records, see Eugene J. Watts, "Police Response to Crime and Disorder in Twentieth-Century St. Louis," *The Journal of American History* (Sept. 1983): 340–58. A colleague and I used municipal reports in two studies of Buenos Aires: Julia Kirk Blackwelder and Lyman L. Johnson, "Changing Criminal Patterns in Buenos Aires, 1890–1914," *Journal of Latin American Studies* (Nov. 1982): 359–79; and "Estadística criminal y acción policial en Buenos Aires, 1887–1914," *Desarrollo Económico* (Abr.-Junio 1984): 109–22.

5. All arrest data in this essay are derived from the following sources: Provincia de Tucumán, *Anuario de Estadística de la Provincia de Tucumán* (Tucumán, 1900–33), Años 1900–30; Sante Fe, Dirección de Estadística Municipal, *Anuario Estadístico de la Ciudad de Sante Fe* (Santa Fe, 1905–1903), Años 1904–1930; Buenos Aires, Dirección General de Estadística, *Anuario Estadístico de la Ciudad de Buenos Aires, 1915–1923* (Buenos Aires, 1925); Buenos Aires, Departamento de Policía, *Memoria, antecedentes, datos estadísticos y crónica de actos públicos* (Buenos Aires, 1925–29) Años 1924–28; and Municipalidad de Buenos Aires, *Revista de estadística municipal*, Año XL, nos. 1–12, and Año XLII, nos. 1–12 (Buenos Aires, 1926–30).

6. Monkkonen, "Municipal Reports," 61.

7. For a comparison between arrests and reported crimes, see Blackwelder and Johnson, "Estadística criminal," 116–17.

8. James R. Scobie, *Buenos Aires: Plaza to Suburb, 1870–1910* (New York, 1974); and Charles S. Sargent, *The Spatial Evolution of Greater Buenos Aires, Argentina, 1870–1930* (Tempe, 1974) are helpful introductions to this topic.

9. República Argentina, *Tercer Censo Nacional* (Buenos Aires, 1918), Tomo 1, 116.

10. For the agricultural revolution and its effect on the city of Sante Fe, see James R. Scobie, *Revolution on the Pampas* (Austin, 1964); Ezequiel Gallo and Roberto Cortés Conde, *Argentina. La Republica Conservadora* (Buenos Aires, 1972); and Ezequiel Gallo, *La pampa gringa. La colonización agrícola en Santa Fe, 1870–1895* (Buenos Aires, 1983). An interesting theoretical argument is offered by Francisco J. Delich in "Tipos de acción y organización campesina en Argentina," in *Revista Paraguaya de Sociología* (Sept. -Dic. 1971): 109–31.

11. Vincente Vazques-Presedo, *Estadísticas Históricas Argentinas* (Buenos Aires, 1971), Primera parte, 26.

12. The development of the sugar industry is summarized in an industry publication, Centro Azucarero Nacional, *La industria azucarera argentina* (Buenos Aires, 1930). Donna Guy has made a significant contribution to our understanding of this industry in two papers: "The Refinería Argentina, 1888–1930: The Limits of Sugar Technology in a Peripheral Economy" (presented to an international symposium on the sugar industry in Latin America and the Caribbean held in Cuervavaca, Mexico, 28 Jan. 1985); and "Sugar Industries at the Periphery of the World Market: Argentina, 1860–1914" (forthcoming in the *Proceedings* of the Conference on the International Cane Sugar Industry).

13. Donna J. Guy, *Argentine Sugar Politics: Tucumán and the Generation of Eighty* (Tempe, 1980), pp. 34–36, 98–99.

14. Vazques-Presedo, *Estadísticas Históricas*, Primera parte, 24–25. See also the excellent city census of 1913, *Censo de la Capital de Tucumán, 1913, Población, Habitación, Industria y Comercio* (Buenos Aires, 1915).

15. Shelly, *Crime and Modernization*, summarizes the theoretical literature in Chapter 1, "Crime in Theoretical Perspective," 3–15. See *Crime and Modernization*, pp. 42–43, for a brief discussion of changes in relationship between property and violent crimes. See also the important statistical analysis by Andrew F. Henry and James F. Short, Jr., *Suicide and Homicide* (Glencoe, Ill. 1954), p. 91.

16. Henry and Short, *Suicide and Homicide*, p. 86.

17. Vazques-Presedo, *Estadísticas Históricas*, Segunda parte, 24–25.

18. Rates for blindness, speech, and hearing impairment are found in República Argentina, *Tercer Censo*, Tomo I, 273–76. In 1914, Buenos Aires and Sante Fe had 50 and 48 blind persons per 1000, respectively. Tucumán

had 147 per 1000. For speech and hearing impairment, Buenos Aires had 61 per 1000, Santa Fe 47 per 1000, anad Tucumán 166 per 1000.

19. Wages and income data are analyzed by Carlos F. Díaz Alejandro, *Essays on the Economic History of the Argentine Republic* (New Haven, 1970), 40–44. See also F. Stack, "Estudio sobre salarios y horarios de los obreros y empleados en los diferentes trabajos de la Capital Federal y en el resto de la República Argentina," *Boletín del Museo Social Argentino*. Tomo III, No. 25–26, pp. 44–49 and No. 29–30, pp. 193–200.

20. Circumstances that influenced the decision to make a misdemeanor arrests are discussed by Eric H. Monkkonen, "A Disorderly People? Urban Order in the Nineteenth and Twentieth Centuries," *Journal of American History* (Dec. 1981): 541–43.

21. For the reform of police in the United States, see Robert M. Fogelson, *Big City Police* (Cambridge, Mass., 1977); and Samuel Walker, *A Critical History of Police Reform: The Emergence of Professionalism* (Lexington, Mass., 1977). The reform of the police department in Buenos Aires is adequately covered by Ramón Cortés Conde, *Historia de la policiá de la ciudad de Buenos Aires*, 2 vols. (Buenos Aires, 1936).

22. Roger Lane made this case for both nineteenth-century Massachusetts and Philadelphia; "Crime and Criminal Statistics in Nineteenth-Century Massachusetts," *Journal of Social History* (Winter 1968): 156–63; and *Violent Death in the City*, p. 120.

23. Monkkonen, "A Disorderly People," 545.

24. Blackwelder and Johnson, "Changing Criminal Patterns," 373–74.

25. Monkkonen, "A Disorderly People," 543.

26. Cortés Conde, *Historia de la policía*, especially Tomo II, 220–46. See also Adolfo Enrique Rodríguez, *Historia de la policía federal argentina*, Tomo VI, 1880–1916 (Buenos Aires, 1980), passim.

27. The effect of these changes in manning priorities are discussed in a comparative context in Blackwelder and Johnson, "Estadística criminal," 119–20.

28. Sargent, *Spatial Evolution of Greater Buenos Aires*, pp. 64–74; and Scobie, *Buenos Aires*, pp. 160–207.

29. Walter F. Willcox, *International Migrations*, Vol. 1, Statistics (New York, 1929), 539–47.

30. A large number of these arrests were of recidivists. Recidivism poses a serious problem for analysis, since published arrest records do not provide information on repeat offenders. See Watts, "Police Response to Crime and Disorder," 341, for a discussion of this problem.

31. Guy, "The Refinería Argentina," 15–23.

32. For the strike of 1923, see Daniel J. Santamaría, *Las huelgas azucareras de Tucumán, 1923* (Buenos Aires, 1984). For the *cañeros* strike, see Daniel

J. Greenberg, "Sugar Depression and Agrarian Revolt: The Argentine Radical Party and the Tucumán *Cañeros* Strike of 1927," *Hispanic American Historical Review* (May, 1987): 301–28.

33. Díaz Alejandro, *Economic History*, p. 37.

34. Carl Solberg discusses the connection between changed economic realities and social conflict in "Rural Unrest and Agrarian Policy in Argentina, 1912–1930," *Journal of Inter-American Studies and World Affairs* (Jan. 1971): 18–52.

35. Harold E. Pepinsky, *Crime Control Strategies: An Introduction to the Study of Crime* (New York, 1980), pp. 33–37.

36. Currently in the state of North Carolina, 70 percent of reported crimes against persons are cleared by an arrest while only 21 percent of crimes against property are cleared. North Carolina Department of Justice, *Crime in North Carolina, 1979* (Raleigh, N.C. 1980), p. 187.

37. Shelley, *Crime and Modernization*, p. 69.

38. This period is well summarized in David Rock, *Politics in Argentina, 1890–1930* (Cambridge, 1975). See also Richard J. Walter, *The Socialist Party of Argentina, 1890–1930* (Austin, 1977); and Julio Godio, *Historia del movimiento obrero argentino* (Buenos Aires, 1972). The connection between political violence and the economic cycle is the subject of an interesting article by Gilbert W. Merkx, "Recessions and Rebellions in Argentina, 1870–1970," in *Hispanic American Historical Review* (May 1973): 285–95.

39. Production of sugar in Tucumán rose from 44,289 tons in 1917 to 325,519 tons in 1927. Centro Azucarero, *La industria azucarera*, p. 44.

40. Santamaría, *Las huelgas*, pp. 12–14. Radical Senator Araoz referred to the "enslaved classes" in a 1920 speech on the labor situation in Tucumán. Cited in Darío Cantón, José L. Moreno, and Alberto Ciria, *Argentina. La democracia constitucional y su crisis* (Buenos Aires, n.d.), pp. 91–92.

41. This point is explored in greater depth in Blackwelder and Johnson, "Changing Criminal Patterns," 367–369.

42. Shelley, *Crime and Modernization*, p. 43, notes that the twenty-five nations with the highest homicide rates are developing nations. Henry and Short, *Suicide and Homicide*, pp. 90–91, find that data from the United States appear to indicate higher rates of violent crime in rural areas.

43. Clarence C. Schrag, "Critical Analysis of Sociological Theories," in Donald J. Mulvihill and Melvin M. Tumin, eds., *Crimes of Violence*, staff report submitted to the National Commission on the Causes and Prevention of Violence, Vol. 13 (Washington D.C., 1969), 1259–66.

44. Joaquín Rubianes, "El retroceso moral de Buenos Aires," *Revista Argentina de Ciencias Políticas* (Ago. 1912): 326–42, are examples of this concern.

45. Blackwelder and Johnson, "Changing Criminal Patterns," 369–71.

46. Roger Lane provides a very useful analysis of existing theory on the social and cultural circumstances that contribute to violence in his conclusion, *Violent Death in the City*, pp. 113–41.

47. Henry and Short, *Suicide and Homicide*, p. 95, find "a positive relation between homicide and the degree of involvement in social or cathectic relationships with other persons."

48. This is an area of research that deserves additional attention. One helpful study is Oscar Yujnovsky, "Políticas de vivienda en la ciudad de Buenos Aires, 1880–1914," *Desarrollo Económico* (Jul.-Sept. 1974): 327–72. See also República Argentina, *Boletín del Departmento Nacional del Trabajo*, "La Habitación," No. 20 (31 Jul. 1912).

49. This argument is made by Enrique R. Aftalión in *La delincuencia en Argentina* (Buenos Aires, 1955), pp. 62–63. He notes that Argentina had a housing deficit of 700,000 units in 1949.

50. Aftalión, *La delincuencia*, p. 89.

51. Roger Lane established an average rate of .27 per 10,000 inhabitants in Philadelphia for the twenty-one-year period 1881–1901. *Violent Death in the City*, p. 60. In 1951, the most murderous region in the United States, East South Central, had a homicide rate of 1.25 per 10,000. Henry and Short, *Suicide and Homicide*, p. 83.

52. Lane, *Violent Death in the City*, p. 102, found that Italian immigrants were the only group indicted at a rate greater than their percentage in the population. Henry and Short, *Suicide and Homicide*, p. 89, cite a 1950 study on age-specific homicide from New Jersey that finds that 64 percent of all homicides were committed by males age thirty-five or younger.

53. This topic has not received very much attention from scholars. An indication of the Latin American experience is provided in a fine study of the Mexican case by María Luisa Rodrigues-Sala de Gomezgil, *Suicidios y suicidas en la sociedad mexicana* (Mexico City, 1974). She found that the peak rate, 1.92 per 10,000, was established in 1952 during a period of substantial internal migration.

54. Lane, *Violent Death in the City*, p. 27.

55. All these rates for the United States, 1910–20, are taken from Rev. Adolph Dominic Frenay, O. P., *The Suicide Problem in the United States* (Boston, 1927), pp. 132–48.

56. Henry and Short, *Suicide and Homicide*, Appendix IV, "The Reaction of Cycles of Suicide to Cycles of Business," pp. 163–73.

57. Walter A. Lunden, *The Suicide Cycle* (Montezuma, Iowa, 1977), p. 182.

58. Between 1919 and 1923, 77 percent of all suicides in Buenos Aires were males. In contrast, during this same period, 57 percent of all attempted suicides were females. Buenos Aires, Dirección General de Estadísticas,

Anuario estadístico de la ciudad de Buenos Aires, 1915–1923, (Buenos Aires, 1925), p. 242.

59. In 1914, more than 55,000 migrants from other provinces were resident in Tucumán. Vazques-Presedo, *Estadísticas Históricas*, Primera parte, p. 23.

60. For comparative wage data, see Díaz Alejandro, *Economic History*, pp. 40–44; and Roberto Cortés Conde, *Tendencias en la evolución de los salarios reales in Argentina, 1880–1910*. Working Paper, Instituto Torcuato DiTella (Buenos Aires, 1975).

Note on Contributors

Lyman L. Johnson is Professor of History at the University of North Carolina at Charlotte.

Susan Midgen Socolow is Professor of History at Emory University.

Richard W. Slatta is Associate Professor of History at North Carolina State University.

Karla Robinson is an independent scholar.

John Charles Chasteen is Assistant Professor of History at Bates College.

Julia Kirk Blackwelder is Associate Professor of History at the University of North Carolina at Charlotte.

Donna J. Guy is Associate Professor of History at the University of Arizona.

Index

abortion, 128
academias de baile, 93
Achaval, Joaquín de, 21
Acosta, Viríssimo, 52–55, 57, 60
adoption, of illegitimate children, 106
adultery, 11–13
Afro-Argentines, control of, 27, 29
Aftalión, Enrique, 110
age: and arrest rates, 76; and crime
   rates, x, xi; and criminal activity,
   22–24; and homicide rates, 137
agregados, property of, 58–59
agriculture: and European markets,
   xii; expansion of, xii, 119;
   provincial, 126–27; and violent
   crime, xviii. *See also* economy,
   Argentine
alcaldes. *See* courts
alcohol: sale of, 20–21, 48; and social
   disorder, 100; and violence, 48–49,
   51–53. *See also* drunkenness;
   pulperías
alienation, of immigrants, 138
Almeida, Ventura, 59–60
Alvear, Torcuato de, 96–97
anarchists, xii, 124
animal control regulations, 21, 82
antisemitism, 124
architecture: of prisons, xii; and social
   interaction, 135; and theft, 69. *See
   also* public buildings
Argentina: economic growth of,
   xii-xiii; immigration to, 66–68
Argentine Congress, 109

Argentine Constitution of 1853, 91
arrest: categories, 121; compared with
   reported crimes, 71; criminal 80; as
   deterrent, 39; discretionary, 125;
   felony, xviii; mass, 97; misdemeanor,
   xviii; patterns, xviii, 35–38, 65, 79;
   statistics, 40–41, 76, 118–19
arrest rates, xi, 35–38; borderland, 51;
   compared with U.S., xi, xvii; and
   criminal activity, 80–81, 128; and
   1890 depression, 79; factors
   affecting, xvi, 36; gambling, 31; and
   gender, 22–24, 29; immigrant, 83;
   for men, 22–24, 73, 76; and
   modernization, 121; and movement
   of population, 139; by nationality,
   77; and police effectiveness, 80; and
   political conflict, 134–35; for
   property crime, 30–31, 121; for
   prostitutes, 107; regression of, 81;
   for scandalous behavior, 108–11;
   seasonal fluctuations in, 37–38; and
   size of police force, 68; and social
   class, 132–33; and social unrest,
   35–36; and type of crime
   committed, 32; urban, 25; for
   violent crime, 30, 129–30; by year, 36
artisans: arrest rates for, 25; honor of,
   55–56
assassination, of police chief, 124
assault, xv; domestic, 119; personal,
   35; physical, 51; rates, 71–72;
   sexual, 7–11, 35; violent, 29
authorities: and borderland violence,

149

www.ingramcontent.com/pod-product-compliance
Lightning Source LLC
Chambersburg PA
CBHW020353270326
41926CB00007B/421